Modern Hindu Thought

Modern Hindu Thought
An Introduction

ARVIND SHARMA

OXFORD
UNIVERSITY PRESS

OXFORD
UNIVERSITY PRESS

YMCA Library Building, Jai Singh Road, New Delhi 110 001

Oxford University Press is a department of the University of Oxford.
It furthers the University's objective of excellence in research,
scholarship, and education by publishing worldwide in

Oxford New York

Auckland Cape Town Dar es Salaam Hong Kong Karachi Kuala Lumpur
Madrid Melbourne Mexico City Nairobi New Delhi Shanghai Taipei Toronto

With offices in

Argentina Austria Brazil Chile Czech Republic France Greece Guatemala
Hungary Italy Japan Poland Portugal Singapore South Korea Switzerland
Thailand Turkey Ukraine Vietnam

Oxford is a registered trademark of Oxford University Press
in the UK and in certain other countries

Published in India by
Oxford University Press, New Delhi

First published 2005

ISBN-13: 978-0-19-567638-9
ISBN-10: 0-19-567638-6

Typeset in Pratap in 10.9/12.7
by Excellent Laser Typesetters, Pitampura, Delhi 110 034
Printed at De-Unique, New Delhi-1100 18.
Published by Manzar Khan, Oxford University Press
YMCA Library Building, Jai Singh Road, New Delhi 110 001

Contents

Introduction

Periodization is a time-honoured method of creating order, or at least a semblance of order, out of chaos, or at least apparent chaos. It was the identification of the 'three-age' system—the Stone Age, Bronze Age, and Iron Age—that first enabled scholars to make sense of the otherwise overwhelming material about the early religious history of humanity, which became available with European expansion over the rest of the world.[1] The point gains credence in the case of a religious tradition such as the Hindu, which is said to glory in its diversity, verging on chaos. Galbraith's description of India as a 'functioning anarchy,' which became 'improbably famous' (in his own words shared at a luncheon in 1995), has even been applied to Hinduism itself with good effect. All this is not as flippant as it sounds. What even Mahatma Gandhi eventually hoped for India, after the end of British rule, was of course, none less than Rāma Rājya in the Hindu idiom but which, when parsed by him into English, emerged as 'ordered anarchy'. It is not for nothing that when Gandhi launched his famous Quit India movement, he asked the British to 'leave India to

[1] Sharpe, Eric J., 'Anthropology', *A Dictionary of Comparative Religion*, S.G.F. Brandon (ed.), New York: Macmillan Publishing Company, 1970, p. 83.

God or anarchy.'[2] Hindu tradition often has trouble distinguishing the two, just as it is prone to confuse bad management with destiny.

The history of such a confusing tradition is bound to be even more so, but just as the British tried to impose some order on India, specially after 1818 when they became the paramount power in the subcontinent, British intellectuals also tried to impose some order on its history, which was undergoing rapid reconstruction at the time. It was around then that James Mill proposed its periodization into the Hindu, Muslim, and British periods.

The classification has stood the test of time. The paradigm did not shift—only the nomenclature changed—when the Hindu, Muslim, and British eras were renamed as the ancient, medieval, and modern periods. In this new classification, the scheme acquired an unconscious or even conscious teleology when modernity, instead of being a temporal description, was inscribed with evolutionary virtue and the modern period then identified with the British.

No such ghost haunts the application of this periodization to the study of Hinduism, wherein a parallel chronology of the religious tradition quickly took shape with its history also being divided into the ancient, medieval, and modern periods. The deepening of the time-horizon with the discovery of the Indus Valley Civilization consolidated the bifurcation of ancient Hinduism as Vedic and post-Vedic, with the result that one now speaks of four periods in the history of Hinduism—the Vedic and pre-Vedic, the classical, the medieval, and the modern.

Some of the underlying concepts of Hinduism can be identified in all four periods, but there is just enough interaction of Hinduism with the non-Vedic elements in the Vedic period; with Buddhism and Jainism in the classical period; with Islam in the medieval period; and with Christianity in the modern period to give Hindu thought in each of these periods a distinctive flavour.

[2] Payne, Robert, *The Life and Death of Mahatma Gandhi*, New York: E.P. Dutton & Co., 1969, p. 494.

This book is devoted to a consideration of modern Hindu thought in this spirit. It is a lineal descendent of an earlier treatment of the theme in *Classical Hindu Thought: An Introduction*, and adopts a similar format.

A word may be in order regarding the limits of the period designated here as modern. Most scholars and readers would presumably be inclined to agree in placing the beginning of the modern period at around c. 1800, by when major changes in the political, social, and religious life of India had begun to occur as a result of European presence in India. Hindus had also by then begun to react to these changes—changes that would ultimately redefine Indian political and religious identities. One might run into difficulties, however, in trying to date the end of the modern period. Its termination could be identified with Indian independence in 1947 and the simultaneous partition of the country. It could, however, also be argued that while the attainment of independence is a watershed in the *political* history of India, the event (although not without significance for the religious history of India) does not affect the operation of the forces in the religious sphere in such a way as to mark the end of a period. Such an event is perhaps to be identified with the acquisition of political power by the Bharatiya Janata party in the 1990s, which introduced an element of Hindu political self-assertion at the national level without easy precedent in the history of Hinduism. I have therefore chosen to work with the 1990s as the cut-off period, after which we enter the phase of contemporary Hinduism.

The book is conceptually divided into three parts. In the first, which constitutes the body of the first chapter, the historical context of modern Hindu thought is delineated. In the second, which constitutes the second chapter, the key concepts of modern Hinduism are presented in relation to each other, until their simultaneous presentation becomes sufficiently coherent to offer a view of modern Hindu thought at a glance, as it were. In the rest of the book, beginning with Chapter 3, each term constitutive of the modern Hindu worldview is successively put under the lens.

PART ONE
The Historical Context

I

The Historical Context

It was noted earlier that it is now customary in the study of Hinduism to divide its long history into distinct periods in order to render its study manageable and that one such widely used scheme demarcates the history of Hinduism into (1) the pre-Vedic and Vedic period; (2) the classical period; (3) the medieval period; and (4) the modern period.[1] There might be differences of opinion regarding the chronological margins of these periods, but the schematic outline is firmly in place.

It was also noted earlier that this book is concerned with the configuration, or reconfiguration, of the key concepts of Hinduism in the modern period. However, intellectual formulations or reformulations do not occur in a vacuum, and are bound to be influenced by the context in which they occur[2] and to which they respond consciously or unconsciously. One does not have to go the lengths of Karl Marx to acknowledge that

[1] Sharma, Arvind (ed.), *The Study of Hinduism*, Columbia, South Carolina: University of South Carolina Press, 2003, pp. ix–x.

[2] For an illustration of how the mundane matter of law may have influenced the socio-religious conceptualization of dowry, see Veena Talwar Oldenberg, *Dowry Murder: The Imperial Origins of a Cultural Crime*, New York: Oxford University Press, 2002.

economic forces might play a role in this process; or of Sigmund Freud to realize that subtle unconscious forces may be involved; or of Michel Foucault to acknowledge the role of institutional frameworks; or of Edward Said to recognize the importance of the colonial context, and so on. The goal of this book is to present the concepts of the tradition at the more manifest level without excavating the economic, psychoanalytical, institutional or Orientalist, or some such sub-text,[3] for the simple reason that there is enough of the text itself to be presented and discussed, to begin with.

Even when one is working at this manifest level, however, it is not possible to gain a full understanding of the intellectual currents that characterize modern Hindu thought without keeping in mind the historical situation in which this process was occurring. This historical situation had certain in-built features that might be helpful to recall, even at the risk of occasionally stating the obvious.

One main feature of this period from the point of view of Hinduism was the fact that it was forced into contact with the West as a result of political developments in the country, just as it had been earlier forced into contact with Islam as a result of political developments. It is helpful to consider here the following typology of responses to Western contact that has been proposed by Ainslie T. Embree. According to him, 'one response was indifference, and this was not purely negative in its results, for it meant that religious and social movements that had their roots in the Hindu tradition continued to flourish.'[4] Embree places Śrī Rāmakṛṣṇa in this category, while acknowledging that even those movements that seem 'completely indigenous in inspiration' could well be 'reflecting a general malaise and unrest caused by the intrusion of the West.'[5] This may be contrasted with 'another and very different

[3] For more on this perspective see David Smith, *Hinduism and Modernity*, Malden, MA: Blackwell Publishing House, 2003.

[4] Embree, Ainslie T. (ed.), *The Hindu Tradition*, New York: Random House, 1972, p. 275.

[5] *Ibid.*, p. 276.

response, [which] was the rejection of the old tradition and the acceptance of everything Western, including Christianity. This attitude was not very common, but it contributed something to the general process of growth and change that characterized the time.'[6] By contrast again, another 'reaction was outright and hostile rejection of the values and ideas of the Western world', although 'here again the range of opinion, and the degree of rejection, varied greatly'.[7] But it was yet another pattern of reaction that was destined to prove more consequential in the long run:

> More common, and of much greater significance, was the reaction to the West that was both critical and selective. Aware of weaknesses within traditional Hindu society, many sought to reform it by using features of Western culture, particularly its political arrangements or its science and technology. This classification covers a very wide spectrum of opinion, including individuals of the most antithetical views, such as Rāmmohan Roy, K.C. Sen, the Tagore family, Vivekānanda, Aurobindo Ghose, Gokhale, Rānade, and Gāndhi.[8]

Certain components of the Western presence in India played a key role in providing the context for such a reconfiguration of Hindu concepts, of which four proved particularly consequential—Christianity and science, and the question of social and political arrangements.

Christianity may not have won as many converts as the missionaries desired, but 'the influence of the Christian gospel radiates out far beyond the limits of the Christian Church.'[9] Modern Hinduism has tended to accept Christ, but not Christianity. A very important dimension of this issue is highlighted in the life of Keshub Chunder Sen (1838–84) during his trip to England. 'During this trip he met Max Mueller, who wrote in a letter to his wife: "We soon got into a warm discussion, and

[6] *Ibid.*

[7] *Ibid.*

[8] *Ibid.*

[9] Neill, Stephen, *The Story of the Christian Church in India and Pakistan*, Grand Rapids, Michigan: William B. Eerdmans Publishing Company, 1970, p. 127.

it was curious to see how we almost made him confess himself a Christian." When asked by Max Mueller why he did not publicly declare himself one, Keshub said: "Suppose that fifty years hence people found out that I was a disciple of Christ, what would be the harm? *Only were I to profess myself a Christian now, all my influence would be gone at once.*"'[10] Yet, Keshub Chunder Sen 'left behind ideas, such as that of Asiatic Christ and of the natural uncongeniality of the gospel to the Western mind, which has almost become a canonical part of modern Hinduism.'[11] In fact, Sen was 'sharply attacked by his own countryman Nehemiah Goreh, the Brahman convert who had become a high church Anglican,'[12] for his concept of the Asiatic Christ. There were some Hindus who became Christians—such people as Reverend Krishnamohan Bandopadhyay, Nehemiah Gore, and Brahmabandhab Upadhyay[13]—and the question arises whether their contribution should be taken into account where the reformulation of Hinduism is concerned. No conscious effort has been made in these pages to include them as representing Hindu thought, since they chose to opt out of the tradition: They should rather be set in the history of Christianity in India. Nor has any special effort been made to include Westerners who, for all intents and purposes, became Hindus—people such as Sister Nivedita and Annie Besant.[14]

This is, however, not to deny that Christian presence influenced Hindu thought. For instance, Christian practice in India arguably influenced Hindu thought by valorizing the category of social service. A.L. Basham, for instance, writes:

> Some precedents for these developments are to be found in the Hinduism of older days. The *Bhagavad Gītā*, as we have seen, inculcates

[10] Sharma, Arvind (ed.), *Modern Hindu Thought: The Essential Texts,* New Delhi: Oxford University Press, 2002, p. 81.

[11] Neill, Stephen, *op. cit.*, p. 122.

[12] *Ibid.*, p. 122.

[13] See Julius J. Lipner, *Brahmabandhab Upadhyay: The Life and Thought of a Revolutionary*, Delhi: Oxford University Press, 1999.

[14] Oldmeadow, Harry, *Journeys East: 20th Century Western Encounters,* Bloomington, Indiana: World Wisdom, 2002, pp. 37–43, 67–9.

ceaseless toil for the welfare of the world, though from the point of view of the author the world's welfare is intimately linked with the strict preservation of the ancient *Dharma.* Some of the devotional poetry of the Middle Ages advocates the service of the poor and suffering as a form of devotion to God. The great fifteenth-century Bengālī reformer, Chaitanya, though a Brāhman, is said to have nursed the sick and aged poor of low caste, even before giving up his home for a life of asceticism when all taboos and caste restrictions cease to apply. The larger temples have always fed the hungry, and often also have cared for the sick in some measure. But the chief impetus to the great development of the social conscience in Hinduism has come from the West.[15]

The question of Hinduism's encounter with modern science constitutes an interesting chapter of modern Hinduism, which deserves a book in itself and can only be addressed briefly here. While other religions, specially Christianity, have a long history of antagonism to science, the experience of Hinduism has been rather different in this respect. There is a tendency even to argue that modern science validates many Hindu concepts (which is really a form of scientism) but the verdict on this point offered by Śrī Chandraśekharendra Sarasvatī (1894–1993), the famous pontiff of Kāñcī, seems to have been accepted by most modern Hindus:

Science is not opposed to religion. It seems to me that it even helps in the growth of religion.[16]

The question of political arrangements during the period of modern Hinduism is as important as it is delicate. Two aspects of the issue stand out—one as an achievement, the other

[15] Basham, A.L., 'Hinduism', *The Concise Encyclopedia of Living Faiths*, R.C. Zaehner (ed.), Boston: Beacon Press, 1972, pp. 255–6. See Gwilym Beckerledge, 'Swami Akandananda's *Sevavrata* (Vow of Service) and the Earliest Expressions of Service to Humanity in the Ramakrishna Math and Mission', in *Gurus and Their Followers: New Religious Reform Movements in Colonial India*, Antony Copley (ed.), New Delhi: Oxford University Press, 2000, pp. 59–82.

[16] Pūjyaśrī Chandraśekharendra Sarasvatī Svāmī, *Hindu Dharma: The Universal Way of Life*, Mumbai: Bharatiya Vidya Bhavan, 1996, p. 146. For more on the point see K.N. Devaraj, *Hinduism and the Modern Age*, New Delhi: Islam and Modern Age Society, 1975.

as a predicament. The achievement consists of the role that democratic ideals have played, and continue to play, in the political sphere. The entire independence movement was predicated on the substitution of British raj by a democratically elected raj. It would be a process to which the instalments of self-government[17] received periodically during British rule itself from early on in the twentieth century also made their contribution, but which came to life when Mahatma Gandhi (after 1920) converted the Congress into a mass-based organization that functioned democratically from within. It was ironically the success of democracy that, according to some observers, may have contributed to Partition, as the Muslim minority became apprehensive of its position in such a democratic set-up. The sheet-anchor against such feared majoritarianism was, of course, the secular state. With the division of the country on religious grounds, however, the concept of the secular state has become the bulwark against majoritarianism in modern India *after* the division of the country, which it failed to prevent. Although this book itself only aims at reviewing the religious and philosophical dimensions of Hinduism in the modern period, it might be worthwhile to cast a glance on the Hindu perceptions of democracy and a secular state—as elements of the religious climate in which the political concepts operate. The possible congruence of the democratic and Hindu way of life may not be difficult to establish;[18] it is the issue of modern Hinduism and the secular state[19] that has become a vexed issue with the rise of political parties in public life that emphasize a Hindu identity.[20] It is worth noting, however, that while these political

[17] Bose, Sugata and Ayesha Jalal, *Modern South Asia: History, Culture, Political Economy*, New Delhi: Oxford University Press, 1998, p. 104 and *passim.*

[18] Sharma, Arvind, 'Hinduism', *Our Religions*, Arvind Sharma (ed.), San Francisco: Harper, 1993, p. 45.

[19] Bhargava, Rajeev, *Secularism and Its Critics*, Delhi: Oxford University Press, 1998.

[20] Jaffrelot, Christophe, *The Hindu Nationalist Movement in India*, New York: Columbia University Press, 1996.

parties have questioned the concept of secularism as it is being applied in India (and labelled it pseudo-secularism), none has questioned the appropriateness of the secular state for a religiously plural country like India. Moreover, even social scientists have noted the potentially hospitable attitude of Hinduism to the concept of a secular state. J. Milton Yinger notes, for instance:

Religious values and structures as well as the secular situation affect the nature of the relationship between church and state. The sharp separation of the duties of Brahmans and Kshatriyas in Hinduism lays the basis for separation of church and state and for the rise of a secular leadership. The lack of an ecclesiastical structure among the Brahmans also supports this development. Their influence being that of individual priests, they have not generally been in a position to challenge secular authority. Thus it has been relatively easy to establish a secular state in India.[21]

One element of Hinduism in the modern era sets it somewhat apart from the immediately preceding period to some extent, but even more sharply from classical Hinduism. Classical Hindu thought is represented by schools of Hindu philosophy such as Nyāya or Vedānta, or the various subsystems of Vedānta, rather than by individual thinkers. There were, of course, influential individual thinkers who belong to the classical period—Udayana, Jayanta, Śaṅkara, and Rāmānuja, to name a few. But they are all associated with specific schools of philosophy. Thus, Hindu thought flowed through the channels of these various schools of philosophy during the classical period.

The picture changes somewhat during the medieval period. While the grand streams of the philosophical systems continued to flow, the personalities of the saint-poets of the Bhakti movement also begin to stand out during this period. This trend towards what we might call individualism becomes more marked during the modern period when, by and large, it is the individual thinkers who begin to count from the time of Raja

[21] Yinger, J. Milton, *The Scientific Study of Religion*, London: The Macmillan Company, 1970, p. 434.

Rammohun Roy (1772/4–1833) onwards.[22] This tendency has achieved a remarkable extension in the post-Independence period, which has witnessed the emergence of a large number of guru-figures in India, many of whom have also gained a substantial following abroad. These individuals have imparted a new spin to certain concepts. Sathya Sai Baba has, for instance, enlarged the role of miracles[23] in the religious context, and Acharya Rajneesh has deepened our understanding of the role of a guru.[24] The full impact of those developments on key Hindu concepts has yet to be assessed—one is too close to the phenomenon, as it were, to analyze it. References have, however, been made to it where appropriate, but there can be little doubt that, in due course, this form of 'guruism'[25] will have important consequences for our understanding of key Hindu categories.

[22] See for instance Arvind Sharma, *The Concept of Universal Religion in Modern Hindu Thought*, London: Macmillan Press Ltd., 1998, wherein the concept of universal religion is discussed not in terms of schools of philosophy but individual thinkers.

[23] See Tal Brooke, *Sai Baba: Lord of the Air*, New Delhi: Vikas Publishing House, 1979.

[24] See Susan J. Palmer and Arvind Sharma, *The Rajneesh Papers: Studies in a New Religious Movement*, Chapter I, Delhi: Motilal Banarsidass, 1993.

[25] This term is used by Axel Michaels to refer to this phenomenon; see Axel Michaels, *Hinduism: Past and Present* (trans. by Barbara Harshav), Princeton and Oxford: Princeton University Press, 2004, p. 46.

PART TWO
A General Introduction

II

A General Introduction

I

The ultimate reality in modern Hinduism is called *Brahman*, as in classical Hinduism. Thus, Rāmakṛṣṇa (1836–86) could still declare: 'Nothing exists except the One. That One is the supreme brahman.'[1] More than before, however, the term *satya* or *sat* has come in vogue to denote the ultimate reality in modern Hinduism. If one chose to distinguish between truth and reality by defining truth as a verbal statement in conformity with reality, then modern Hindu usage has obliterated the distinction, and the word satya is used to refer to both truth and reality. This may represent the acceptance of the correspondence theory of truth with a vengeance! It might also represent elements of the medieval heritage in which satya, sat, and *satnām* gained prominence as words denoting the ultimate during the medieval period (c. 1000–1800) in the history of Hinduism, and the word brahman was used less frequently although it did not go out of currency. Another element that may have encouraged this trend is the popular

[1] Swami Nikhilananda (tr.), *The Gospel of Sri Ramakrishna*, New York: Ramakrishna-Vivekananda Center, 1952, p. 242.

description of brahman as *saccidānanda*, and the occasional tendency of adjectives to become substantives.

In philosophical discussions, however, as distinguished from more general ones, brahman remains the preferred word for the ultimate reality in modern Hinduism.

Hence, the first episteme for understanding modern Hinduism is brahman (satya).

II

The time-honoured distinction between *nirguṇa* and *saguṇa* brahman continues to be important, but is somewhat less significant in the context of modern Hinduism as compared to the classical. 'The main issue that was debated by the Vedāntins who came after Śaṅkara [ninth century] was whether brahman was nirguṇa or saguṇa.'[2] The echoes of the debate can be heard in modern Hinduism, but it has taken on a distinctly academic tone with a growing recognition that the issue is not one of brahman being either this or that, but of it being both.

The extreme positions, although they do not dominate the debate, continue to be represented. Ramaṇa Maharṣi (1879–1950) continues the tradition of emphasizing the nirguṇa aspect, and Devendranath Tagore (1817–1905) the saguṇa aspect. The favoured modern Hindu terms employed in English to refer to nirguṇa and saguṇa brahman are Impersonal God and Personal God respectively. Ramaṇa Marharṣi offers a masterly metaphysically graded summation from the absolutistic perspective as follows:

> The *ajāta* school of Advaita says, 'Nothing exists except the one reality. There is no birth or death, no projection or drawing in, no *sādhaka*

[2] Mahadevan, T.M.P., *Outlines of Hinduism*, Bombay: Chetana Limited, 1971, p. 150. In medieval Hinduism, the distinction between nirguṇa and saguṇa was extended to attitudes of devotion to Īśvara or saguṇa brahman itself, see Ainslie T. Embree (ed.), *Sources of Indian Tradition*, New York: Columbia University Press, 1988, pp. 343–4, 371.

(practiser), no *mumukshu* (one who desires to be liberated), no *mukta* (one who is liberated), no bondage, no liberation. The one unity alone exists for ever.' To such as find it difficult to grasp this truth and ask 'How can we ignore this solid world we see all around us?' the dream experience is pointed out and they are told, 'All that you see depends on the seer. Apart from the seer there is no seen.' This is called *drishti-srishti vāda* or the argument that one first creates out of his mind and then sees what his mind itself has created.[3]

He goes on to say:

To such as cannot grasp even this and who further argue: 'The dream experience is so short, while the world always exists. The dream experience was limited to me. But the world is felt and seen not only by me but by so many and we cannot call such a world non-existent,' the argument called *srishti-drishi vāda* is addressed and they are told, 'God first created such and such a thing out of such and such an element and then something else and so forth.' That alone will satisfy them. Their mind is not otherwise satisfied and they ask themselves 'How can all geography, all maps, all sciences, stars, planets and the rules governing or relating to them, and all knowledge be totally untrue?' To such it is best to say: 'Yes. God created all this and so you see it'. All these are only to suit the capacity of the hearers. The absolute can only be one.[4]

On the other hand, someone like Devendranath Tagore had little use for the kind of absolutism associated with Śaṅkara and elaborated above by Ramaṇa. His biographer, Narayan Chaudhuri, points out that Devendranath revived the Brāhmo Dharma after Rammohun Roy and insisted that

the worshipped-worshipper relation between God and His devotee is the basis of Brahmo Dharma. Now, if instead of this a relation subsists between the worshipped and the worshipper which equates God with His devotee, the ego of the worshipper is pampered beyond measure and the whole structure of Brahmo Dharma falls to the ground. Let me quote below the actual words of the Autobiography in translation: 'But 'I am myself God'—such kind of self-gloating is the source of much evil. One should stop uttering such words. What can be more surprising than

[3] Mudaliar, A. Devaraj (compiler), *Gems from Bhagavan*, Tiruvannamalai: Sri Ramanasramam, 1978, pp. 3–4, diacritics supplied.

[4] *Ibid.* Also see *The Teachings of Ramana Maharshi*, David Godman (ed.), London and New York: Arkana, 1985, pp. 181–3.

that a man should regard himself as everlastingly free when in fact he is bound by a hundred ties of worldly attachments and entangled in infirmities, bereavements, sins, sorrows, etc.? Shankaracharya has turned the head of India by preaching equation between Jiva and Brahma. Under his spell the sannyasins and even householders are uttering this nonsense 'So'ham': 'I am God!' (Chapter 28).[5]

This position was maintained by his son Rabindranath Tagore (1861–1941). D.S. Sarma offers a remarkably lucid and balanced account of the role of these two conceptions of Brahman in modern Hinduism as found in the context of Tagore's thought as follows: 'It is well known that the Upanishads speak of both the personal and the impersonal aspects of God. The personal aspects gave rise later to Vedantic theism, and the impersonal aspects to Vedantic absolutism.... Tagore, in his Hibbert lectures, makes mention of both the views and his own choice. He does not deny the truth of the absolutist view. In that respect he is more liberal than his father but he thinks that, for the Religion of Man, the theistic view alone is of any value.'[6]

In their own way, however, these extremes tend to meet in mainline modern Hinduism. This is evident if we consider the views of an absolutist such as Ramaṇa Maharṣi and a theist like Mahatma Gandhi. 'Sri Ramana maintained that the universe is sustained by the power of the Self. Since theists normally attribute this power to God he often used the word God as a synonym for the Self. He also used the word *Brahman*, the supreme being of Hinduism, and Siva, a Hindu name for God, in the same way. Sri Ramana's God is not a personal God, he is the formless being which sustains the universe. He is not the creator of the universe, the universe is merely a manifestation of his inherent power; he is inseparable from it, but he is not affected by its appearance or its disappearance'.[7] Mahatma Gandhi provides the foil: 'I am an *advaitist* and yet

[5] Chaudhuri, Narayan, *Maharshi Devendranath Tagore*, New Delhi: Sahitya Akademi, 1973, p. 40.

[6] Sarma, D.S., *Hinduism Through the Ages*, Bombay: Bharatiya Vidya Bhavan, 1956, pp. 175–6.

[7] Godman, David, *op. cit.*, p. 10.

I support *dvaitism* (dualism). The world is changing every moment and is therefore unreal, it has no permanent existence. But though it is constantly changing, it has something about it which persists and it is therefore to that extent real.'[8] He goes on to say:

From the platform of the Jains I prove the non-creative aspect of God, and from that of Ramanuja the creative aspect. As a matter of fact we are all thinking of the Unthinkable, describing the Indescribable, seeking to know the Unknown, and that is why our speech falters, is inadequate and even often contradictory. That is why the *Vedas* describe *Brahman* as 'not this', 'not this'. But if He or It is not this, He or It *is*. If we exist, if our parents and their parents have existed, then it is proper to believe in the Parent of the whole creation. If He is not, we are nowhere. And that is why all of us with one voice call one God differently as *Paramatma*, *Ishwara*, Shiva, Vishnu, Rama, Allah, *Khuda*, Dada Hormuzda, Jehova, God, and an infinite variety of names. He is one and yet many; He is smaller than an atom, and bigger than the Himalayas. He is contained even in a drop of the ocean, and yet not even the seven seas can encompass Him.[9]

There is a distinct tendency in modern Hinduism to reconcile the different concepts of brahman with the different schools of Hindu thought related to Vedānta. This tendency manifests itself both at the experiential and the academic level. Rāmakṛṣṇa declared:

MASTER: 'Again, I cannot utter a word unless I come down at least two steps from the plane of samādhi. *Śaṅkara's Non-dualistic explanation of Vedānta is true, and so is the Qualified Non-dualistic interpretation of Rāmānuja.*'

NARENDRA: 'What is Qualified Non-dualism?'

MASTER: 'It is the theory of Rāmānuja. According to this theory, Brahman, or the absolute, is qualified by the universe and its living beings. These three—Brahman, the world, and living beings—together constitute One. Take the instance of a bel-fruit. A man wanted to know the weight of the fruit. He separated the shell, the flesh, and the seeds. But can a man get the weight by weighing only the flesh? He must weigh flesh, shell,

[8] M.K. Gandhi, *Hindu Dharma*, Ahmedabad: Navajivan Publishing House, 1950, p. 55.

[9] *Ibid.*, pp. 55–6, with 'compass' modified to 'encompass.'

and seeds together. At first it appears that the real thing in the fruit is the flesh, and not its seeds or shell. Then by reasoning you find that the shell, seeds, and flesh all belong to the fruit; the shell and seeds belong to the same thing that the flesh belongs to. Likewise, in spiritual discrimination one must first reason, following the method of 'Not this, not this': God is not the universe; God is not the living beings; Brahman alone is real and all else is unreal. Then one realizes, as with the bel-fruit, that the Reality from which we derive the notion of Brahman is the very Reality that evolves the idea of living beings and the universe. The Nitya and the Līlā are the two aspects of one and the same Reality; therefore, according to Rāmānuja, Brahman is qualified by the universe and the living beings. This is the theory of Qualified Non-dualism.'[10]

Rāmakṛṣṇa's response is positive; Ramaṇa's, while more tentative, is equally tolerant:

D.: The final state of Realization is said, according to Advaita, to be absolute union with the Divine, and according to Visishtadvaita a qualified union, while Dvaita maintains that there is no union at all. Which of these should be considered the correct view?

B.: Why speculate about what will happen some time in the future? All are agreed that the 'I' exists. To whichever school of thought he may belong, let the earnest seeker first find out what the 'I' is. Then it will be time enough to know what the final state will be, whether the 'I' will get merged in the Supreme Being or stand apart from Him. Let us not forestall the conclusion, but keep an open mind.[11]

Thus, whereas in classical Hinduism there was a strong general tendency to give primacy to one formulation of Brahman over the other, modern Hinduism tends to recognize their coordination rather than subordination. A sense of exclusion regarding the two aspects is less marked therein. This may in part be the result of the more nonsectarian character of modern Hinduism compared to the classical, and also in part because of the renewed emphasis placed on tolerance in modern Hinduism. Religious tolerance is present as an element in Hinduism throughout its history, but the

[10] Swami Nikhilananda (tr.), *op. cit.*, pp. 733–4, diacritics supplied.

[11] Osborne, Arthur (ed.), *The Teachings of Bhagavan Sri Raman Maharshi in His Own Words*, Tiruvannamalai: Sri Ramanasramam, 1971, p. 55. *D.* = devotee, *B.* = Bhagavān Ramaṇa.

emphatic accent placed on it belongs to modern Hinduism, for which classical sources are freely used as prooftexts.

This approximation of the two forms of brahman can be detected both in modern Hindu philosophy and modern Hindu religiosity. S. Radhakrishnan explains:

> We thus get the conception of an Absolute-God, *Brahman–Īśvara*, where the first term indicates infinite being and possibility, and the second suggests creative freedom. Why should the Absolute Brahman—perfect, infinite, needing nothing, desiring nothing—move out into the world? It is not compelled to do so. It may have this potentiality but it is not bound or compelled by it. It is free to move or not to move, to throw itself into forms or remain formless. If it still indulges its power of creativity, it is because of its free choice.[12]

* * *

> The distinction between *Brahman* in itself and *Brahman* in the universe, the transcendent beyond manifestation and the transcendent in manifestation, the indeterminate and the determinate, *nirguṇo guṇī*, is not exclusive. The two are like two sides of one reality. The Real is at the same time being realised.[13]

* * *

> The *nirākāra* (formless), and the *sākāra* (with form), are different aspects of the same Reality.[14]

Saguṇa brahman is distinguished from nirguṇa brahman on account of its association with *māyā*, which in its creative aspect is also called *śakti*. Rāmakṛṣṇa proclaimed:

> I have realized that brahman and śakti are identical, like water and its wetness, like fire and its power to burn.[15]

[12] Radhakrishnan, S. (ed.), *The Principal Upaniṣads*, London: George Allen & Unwin, 1953, p. 63.

[13] *Ibid.*, p. 70.

[14] *Ibid.*, p. 71.

[15] Swami Nikhilananda (tr.), *op. cit.*, p. 550. In fact, Rāmakṛṣṇa is said to have disabused his nirguṇa-oriented Advaitic master Totāpurī of a misunderstanding on this score, see Swami Saradananda, *The Great Master*, Swami Jagadananda (tr.), Madras: Sri Ramakrishna Math, 1952, pp. 485–9.

There is a certain fluidity that characterizes modern Hinduism in respect to the manner in which the ultimate reality is characterized. The different characterizations of the experiences of Rāmakṛṣṇa within the literature of the Rāmakṛṣṇa Mission bear interesting testimony to this fact. One can point to an Advaitizing tendency as to a theitizing one, and the following comment presents in a compact way the welter of forces impinging on this fluidity, which argues that 'in light of Swami Vivekananda's advocacy of Advaita Vedānta philosophy, it appears that he and members of the movement—the Rāmakṛṣṇa math and mission—became embarrassed by Rāmakṛṣṇa's devotion to Kālī and wanted to expunge her as much as possible and to correct their master by referring to ultimate reality in neutral or masculine rather than feminine terms.'[16]

In contrast to an absolutizing tendency, Hinduism displays a theistic tendency, which is different from saying that it is theistic. The Absolute has not been banished from it but, instead of treating it as apart from God, there is stronger tendency to associate it with God. This might be seen as the continuation of an earlier trend. For 'during the late Middle Ages when the Bhakti movement swept over the entire country, even the adherents of the so-called path of knowledge (chiefly the Advaita-Vedāntins, e.g. Madhusudan Sarasvati) felt drawn towards devotional practices.'[17]

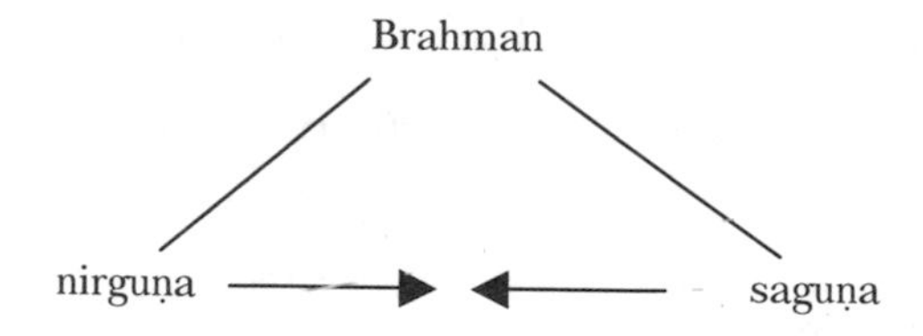

[16] Olson, Carl, *The Mysterious Play of Kālī: An Interpretive Study of Rāmakṛṣṇa*, Atlanta, Georgia: Scholars Press, 1990, p. X. For an appraisal of what went in and what came out of Vivekānanda's Advaita, see Thomas Mannumel, S.J., *The Advaita of Vivekananda: A Philosophical Appraisal*, Madras: T.R. Publications Pvt. Ltd., 1991.

[17] Devaraja, N.K., *Hinduism and the Modern Age*, New Delhi: Islam and the Modern Age Society, 1975, p. 4.

III

The triume description of Brahman as saccidānada has assumed almost greater significance in modern Hinduism than the Hindu trinity of Brahmā, Viṣṇu, and Śiva. This is apparent in both the absolutistic and the theistic aspects of Hinduism. The expression is used so freely by the absolutist Ramaṇa Maharṣi that the compiler of his teachings is compelled to provide the following note on it:

This is a Sanskrit term which translates as being-consciousness-bliss. Sri Ramana taught that the self is pure being, a subjective awareness of 'I am' which is completely devoid of the feeling 'I am this' or 'I am that'. There are no subjects or objects in the Self, there is only an awareness of being. Because this awareness is conscious it is also known as consciousness. The direct experience of this consciousness is, according to Sri Ramana, a state of unbroken happiness and so the term *ananda* or bliss is also used to describe it. These three aspects, being, consciousness, and bliss—are experienced as a unitary whole and not as separate attributes of the Self. They are inseparable in the same way that wetness, transparency and liquidity are inseparable properties of water.[18]

The metaphysical depth in the absolutistic context of the use of sat and *cit* (*ānanda* having been covered in the previous citation) becomes clear from the following excerpt of Ramaṇa's conversations:

...What is the standard of Reality? That alone is Real which exists by itself, which reveals itself by itself, and which is eternal and unchanging.

Does the world exist by itself? Was it ever seen without the aid of the mind? In sleep there is neither mind nor world. When awake there is the mind and there is the world. What does this invariable concomitance mean? You are familiar with the principles of inductive logic, which are considered the very basis of scientific investigation. Why do you not decide this question of the reality of the world in the light of those accepted principles of logic?

Of yourself you can say 'I exist.' That is, yours is not mere existence; it is Existence of which you are conscious. Really, it is Existence identical with Consciousness.

[18] Godman, David, *op. cit.*, pp. 9–10.

D. The world may not be conscious of itself, yet it exists.

M. Consciousness is always Self-consciousness. If you are conscious of anything, you are essentially conscious of yourself. Unself-conscious existence is a contradiction in terms. It is no existence at all. It is merely attributed existence, whereas true Existence, the *sat,* is not an attribute, it is the Substance itself. It is the *vastu.* Reality is therefore known as *sat-chit,* Being-Consciousness, and never merely the one to the exclusion of the other. The world neither exists by itself, nor is it conscious of its existence. How can you say that such a world is real?

And what is the nature of the world? It is perpetual change, a continuous, interminable flux. A dependent, unself-conscious, ever-changing world cannot be real.[19]

The theistic implication of the triume description is best explained with the help of Mahatma Gandhi's statements about it. He explains: 'The word satya (Truth) is derived from sat, which means "being". Nothing is or exists in reality except Truth. That is why sat or Truth is perhaps the most important name of God. In fact it is more correct to say that Truth is God, than to say that God is Truth. But as we cannot do without a ruler or a general, names of God such as "King of Kings" or "the Almighty" are and will remain generally current. On deeper thinking, however, it will be realized, that sat or satya is the only correct and fully significant name for God.'[20] Gandhi's explanation is strongly theological, rather than metaphysical. This becomes increasingly obvious as he proceeds to explain the other terms. 'And where there is Truth, there also is knowledge which is true. Where there is no Truth, there can be no true knowledge. That is why the word *Chit* or knowledge is associated with the name of God. And where there is true knowledge, there is always bliss (Ānanda). There sorrow has no place. And even as Truth is eternal, so is the bliss derived from it. Hence we know God as *Sat-chit-ananda,* One who combines in Himself Truth, Knowledge and Bliss.'[21]

[19] Miller, Joe & Guinevere (eds), *The Spiritual Teaching of Ramana Maharshi,* Boston and London: Shambhala, 1988, pp. 89–90.

[20] M.K. Gandhi, *op. cit.,* p. 221.

[21] *Ibid.*

In this context it cannot be sufficiently emphasized that Truth for Gandhi is as much a metaphysical as a moral principle.

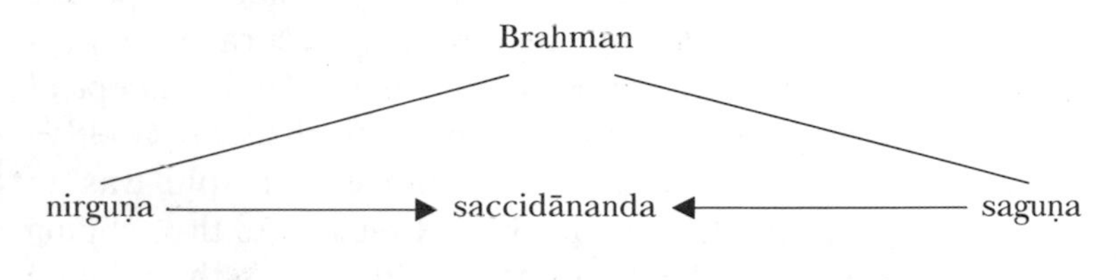

IV

The expression saccidānanda serves to link the concepts of nirguṇa and saguṇa brahman or Íśvara in modern Hinduism and represents the trend that tends to look on these two aspects as two sides of the same coin. From this point of view, the thinking around the ultimate in terms of the feminine principle represents something of a departure. The worship of the Goddess in its own right doubtless continues to flourish. The lives of Rāmakṛṣṇa[22] and Vivekananda[23] provide ample testimony in this respect.

However, as the ultimate concerns of modern Hinduism began to be choreographed in the light of contemporary forces, it displayed three somewhat surprising applications of this principle.

First, as nationalism rose in response to British imperialism in India, it affected the religious sensibilities of the Hindus by being directed, at least initially, in a religious direction. Thus emerged the vision of *Mother India*. The person who moved the Hindu imagination perhaps most in this direction is Bankim Chandra Chatterjee (1838–94), for 'the poem *Bande Mātaram* (*Hail to the Mother*) which first appeared in one of his novels soon became the *Marseillaise* of the nationalist movement

[22] See Carl Olson, *op. cit., passim.*

[23] See George M. Williams, *The Quest for Meaning of Svāmī Vivekānanda: A Study in Religious Change*, Chico, California: New Horizons Press, 1974, p. 28ff; *The Complete Works of Sister Nivedita*, Part I, Calcutta: Ramakrishna Sarada Mission, 1967, p. 467ff.

throughout the country.'[24] Scholars note that 'Bankim's original concept, "the Mother" of *Bande Mātaram*, referred at the same time to the land of Bengal and to the female aspect of the Hindu deity. From the fusion of the hitherto separate objects of patriotic and religious devotion.... sprang the central concept of modern Hindu nationalism.' This concept of divine motherhood equated "love of country with love of God."'[25]

The second extension of the feminine principle was to Hinduism itself, and then by further extension, to the religion one was *born in*. The idea that one should stick to the religion one is born in[26] is a major ingredient of modern Hinduism. This position was expressed in a message sent by Mahatma Gandhi to a Parliament of Religions: 'What will the Parliament of Religions say in respect of all religions? Are all religions equal, as we hold, or is any particular religion in the sole possession of truth and the rest either untrue or a mixture of truth and error as many believe? The opinion of the Parliament in such matters must prove a helpful guidance.'[27]

In response, Sir Francis Younghusband said:

> To Mahatma Gandhi's question I would add another question: Are all mothers equally good? All mothers are not equally good, but each would think his own mother as the best in the world. Similarly, each one would regard his own religion as the best in the world. At any rate, that was certainly the impression that he gained at the World Congress of Faiths last year. Each one did honestly believe that his religion was the best. I have come in very close contact with people of diverse faiths and have discovered a fundamental unity among all these religions. It is this fundamental unity which I desire this Congress to realize and deepen and make it permanent and abiding.[28]

The third extension of the feminine principle was its application to the Bhagavadgītā. Mahatma Gandhi remarked: 'I run to my mother *Gītā* whenever I find myself in difficulties, and

[24] de Bary, Wm. Theodore (ed.), *Sources of Indian Tradition*, Vol. II, New York and London: Columbia University Press, 1958, p. 156.

[25] *Ibid.*, p. 156. Also see p. 107.

[26] M.K. Gandhi, *op. cit.*, p. 232.

[27] *Ibid.*, p. 235.

[28] *Ibid.*

up to now she has never failed to comfort me.'[29] Elsewhere, he said: 'Whenever under stress we hasten to the Gītā for relief and obtain consolation, it is at once for us a teacher—a mother, and we must have faith that with our head in her lap we shall always remain safe.'[30] In fact Vinoba Bhave, one of Gandhi's well known followers, refers to the Gītā as *Gītāī*[31] in Marathi, that is to say, *Mother Gītā.*

The manner in which the authority of the Bhagavadgītā came to be established within modern Hinduism is not without interest. The Gītā is not a part of *śruti* or revelation proper in Hinduism, and yet has come to enjoy at least a similar status and is certainly more widely known than the Vedas. An intriguing possibility is presented by Rāmakṛṣṇa's approach to the question of scriptural authority that could enable the Gītā to be placed above the Vedas. Rāmakṛṣṇa distinguishes between two interpretations of scriptures—'the literal and the real'. He goes on to say: 'There is a vast difference between the words written in a letter and the direct words of its writer. The scriptures are like the words of the letter; the words of God are direct words.' Then, he adds: 'I do not accept anything unless it agrees with the direct words of the divine mother.' If we now backtrack a bit and regard the Vedas as 'words of the letter'[32] and the Gītā as 'direct words of God', where does that take us? At the moment, it leads us into the next section.

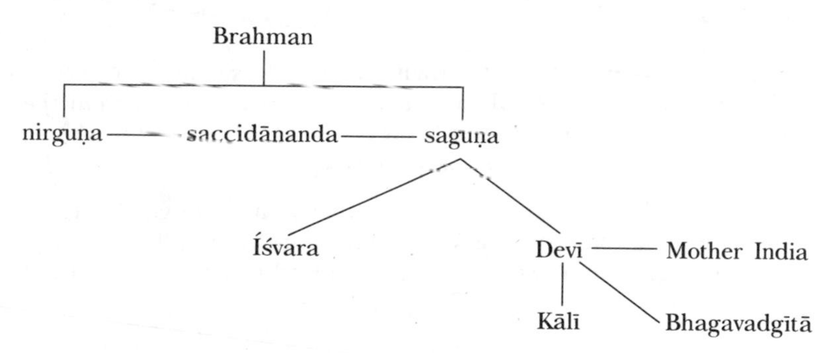

[29] *Ibid.*
[30] *Ibid.*
[31] *Ibid.*, p. 161.
[32] Swami Nikhilananda (tr.), *op. cit.*, pp. 772–3.

V

The next issue that needs to be tackled in any discussion on the essentials of modern Hinduism is incarnation.

In the early phase of modern Hinduism, there emerged a growing tendency to deny incarnation—in contrast to classical Hinduism wherein the doctrine is a vital one, especially as relating to Viṣṇu. Gradually, however, two interrelated phenomena diffused the issue. On the one hand, the issue itself subsided, and on the other, fresh interpretations of the doctrine surfaced in neo-Hinduism.

The issue may be personalized in the context of the interaction of Vivekananda and Rāmakṛṣṇa to lend it some vigour. George Willaims has drawn attention to the fact that, as late as 11 March 1885, the would-be Swami Vivekananda, like the Brāhmo Samājists, did not believe in incarnation.[33] By 27 October 1885, however, he had come round to the view that just as 'there is a point between the vegetable creation and the animal creation where it is very difficult to determine whether a particular thing is a vegetable or an animal'[34] so might it be in relation to someone in-between man-world and God-world.

By January 1886, Vivekananda was willing to identify 'Rāmakṛṣṇa as an *avatāra* of śakti.'[35] Then followed the denouement:

> In August 1886, Rāmakṛṣṇa's final self-revelation was made to Narendra on his deathbed. It is recalled in a later account derived from the community of devotees, but most likely reflects his beliefs at this time. The narrative reconstructs this last question:
>
> > He has said many times that he is an incarnation of God. If I can make him say now as he is in the throes of death, in the midst of human anguish and physical pain, 'I am God incarnate,' then I will believe him!

[33] Williams, George M., *The Quest for Meaning of Svāmī Vivekānanda*, p. 31.

[34] *Ibid.*

[35] *Ibid.*

The moment this thought came to Narendra's mind, it was stated that Rāmakṛṣṇa declared: 'O my Naren, are you not yet convinced? He who was Rama and Krishna is now Rāmakṛṣṇa in this body—but not from the standpoint of your Vedanta.'

It does not come as a surprise that Narendra and the gurubhāis worshipped Rāmakṛṣṇa after his mahāsamādhi as a Deity.[36]

It is perhaps a coincidence, though an interesting one, that in modern Hinduism the two incarnations of Viṣṇu that play the most significant role out of his ten incarnations of classical Hinduism are those of Rāma and Kṛṣṇa. But though Rāma and Kṛṣṇa continue to remain the two most significant incarnations, the nature of their significance differs somewhat. This is a point we shall advert to later. At this stage, it would be appropriate to indicate how modern Hinduism tries to handle the issue of incarnation by modifying the concept itself in various ways.

Aurobindo Ghose (1872–1950) suggests that whereas God incarnated himself as or in an individual form in earlier ages, he may now incarnate himself in a society or a people rather than as an individual: '...when God is going to be born in a people';[37] Mahatma Gandhi (1869–1948) regards the perfection of an avatāra such as Kṛṣṇa as existing in one's 'imagination',[38] and holds the same view regarding Rāma.[39] Pratima Bowes sees in this doctrine the reflection of the broader principle that 'God is present in everything but his essence is manifested more in some things than in others—things which possess excellence or perfection to a striking degree;'[40] K.M. Sen observes shrewdly that 'while some Hindus take the doctrine literally and accept figures like Rāma, Kṛishṇa, and Buddha as actual incarnations, others prefer to treat it as a useful myth;'[41] many rationalist Hindus read in the sequence

[36] *Ibid.*, pp. 31–2.

[37] de Bary, Wm. Theodore (ed.), *op. cit.*, Vol. II, p. 177.

[38] M.K. Gandhi, *op. cit.*, p. 18.

[39] *Ibid.*, p. 9.

[40] Bowes, Pratima, *The Hindu Religious Tradition: A Philosophical Approach*, London: Routledge & Kegan Paul, 1977, p. 220.

[41] Sen, K.M. *Hinduism*, Harmondsworth: Penguin, 1963, p. 73 note 1.

of the early incarnations 'a suggestion regarding the order of biological evolution',[42] while S. Radhakrishnan remarks: 'The incarnation is not a special event but a continuous process of self-renewal.'[43] Aurobindo Ghose spreads it out in space, Radhakrishnan spreads it out in time!

As indicated earlier, the most significant incarnations of Viṣṇu, are those of Rāma and Kṛṣṇa. The popularity of Rāma was recently attested to by the astonishing success of the TV series based on his life[44], and earlier by Mahatma Gandhi's famous *bhajan.*[45] It may also rest on Rāma's 'role as a model of human behaviour', as indicated by the popular epithet *maryādā-puruṣottama-śrīrāma.*[46] In modern Hinduism, especially after the rise of Indian nationalism, Rāma became symbolic of the victory of right over might—the latter being represented by British rule. Telling use of a passage from the *Rāmacaritamānasa* was made by Mahatma Gandhi in which an ostensibly weak Rāma takes on the mighty Rāvaṇa, a typical David-Goliath contest, on the basis of moral heroism. Thus, the chariot with which Rāma was to defeat Rāvaṇa is not seen so much as a physical but rather as a moral construct:

> To sum up, the equipment of a *satyagrahi* soldier will consist not of weapons of steel but those of the spirit. In *Tulsi Ramayana*, Vibhishan asks Rama as to what the real equipment of a satyagrahi army is that leads to victory. Rama had 'no chariot, no armour, nor any shoes to his feet.' Then how did he expect to win against Ravan, who had all these? To him Rama replies:
>
> > The chariot, my dear Vibhishan, that wins the victory for Rama is of a different sort from the usual one. Manliness and courage are its wheels; unflinching truth and character its banners and standards;

[42] Swami Nirvedananda, *Hinduism at a Glance*, Calcutta: Ramakrishna Mission, 1969, p. 135.

[43] Radhakrishnan, S. (tr.), *The Brahman Sūtra: The Philosophy of the Spiritual Life*, London: George Allen &Unwin, 1960, p. 174.

[44] Richman, Paula (ed.), *Questioning Rāmāyaṇas: A South Asian Tradition*, Berkeley: University of California Press, 2000, p. 360 note 5.

[45] Mahadevan, T.M.P., *op. cit.*, p. 274.

[46] Goldman Robert P. (tr.), *The Rāmāyaṇa of Vālmīki*, Vol. I, Princeton, New Jersey: Princeton University Press, 1984, p. 42.

strength, discrimination, self-restraint and benevolence its horses, with forgiveness, mercy, equanimity as their reins; prayer to God is that conqueror's unerring charioteer, dispassion his shield, contentment his sword, charity his axe, intellect his spear, and perfect science his stout bow. His pure and unwavering mind stands for a quiver, his mental quietude and his practice of *yama* and *niyama* stand for the sheaf of arrows, and the homage he pays to Brahmans and his *guru* is his impenetrable armour. There is no other equipment for victory comparable to this; and my dear friend, there is no enemy who can conquer the man who takes his stand on the chariot of *dharma*. He who has a powerful chariot like this is a warrior who can conquer even that great and invincible enemy—the world. Hearken unto me and fear not.[47]

This appropriation of Rāma as a heroic fighter for righteousness has precedents in classical and medieval Hinduism (sometimes surprisingly ignored[48]) and hence does not hold much surprise. It is Kṛṣṇa whom modern Hinduism has appropriated somewhat differently. The Kṛṣṇa of classical and especially medieval Hinduism was more associated with dalliance with the *gopīs* than with the role played by him in the context of the Bhagavadgītā; and the Bhagavadgītā was itself understood as conveying the message of *jñāna* or *bhakti* rather than *karma*. The heroic mould of Kṛṣṇa's character was recovered in modern Hinduism by emphasizing his connection with the Bhagavadgītā. This produced far-reaching consequences: first, the Bhagavadgītā came to be accepted as virtually *the* scripture of Hinduism[49] and, second, its message came to be interpreted along activistic lines.[50]

Another major change that characterizes Hinduism is the positive reappropriation of the Buddha (and thereby of

[47] Pyarelal, *Mahatma Gandhi: The Last Phase*, Vol. II, Ahmedabad: Navajivan Publishing House, 1958, p. 621.

[48] Goldman, Robert P. (tr.), *The Ramāyaṇa of Vālmīki*, p. 46 note 90 wherein the coincidence between the evidence of a Rāma cult starting only from the eleventh century, and the establishment of Muslim rule over India is ignored. See Sheldon Pollock, 'Rāmāyaṇa and Political Imagination in India', in *The Journal of Asian Studies*, 52:2:261–97, 1993.

[49] Sharpe, Eric J., *The Universal Gītā*, London: Duckworth, 1985, p. 83.

[50] *Ibid.*, pp. 83–5.

Buddhism). Once virtually banished as the illegitimate child of Hinduism, the Buddha was now welcomed home as the prodigal son by modern Hinduism,[51] and has virtually displaced Balarāma in the traditional listing of the Ten Incarnations.

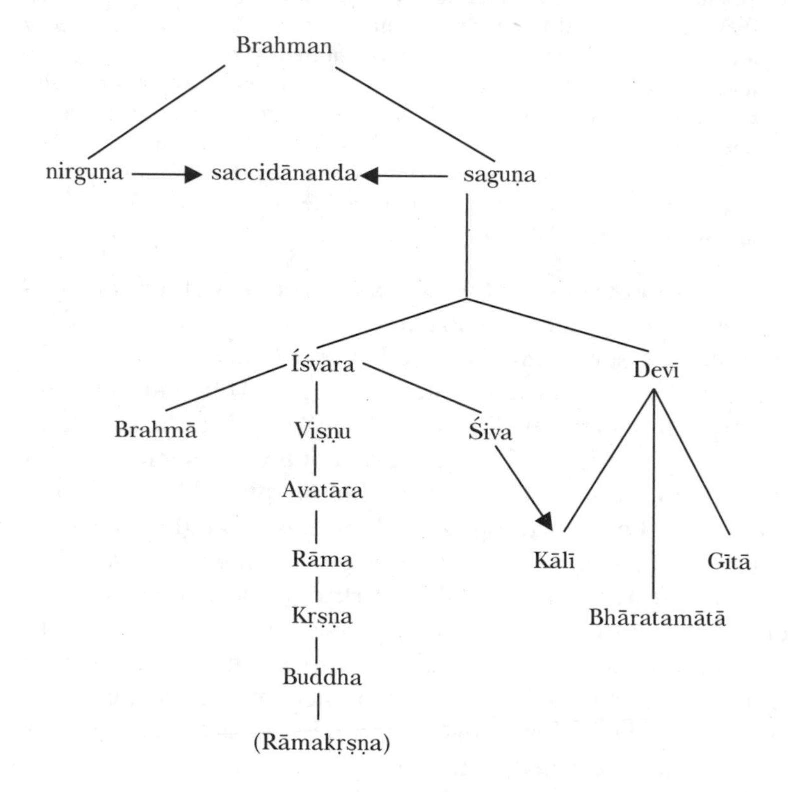

[51] See Hendrik Kraemer, *World Cultures and World Religions: The Coming Dialogue,* London: Lutterworth Press, 1960, p. 163: 'India, from which Buddhism since the 11th century had disappeared and was forgotten, began to enter again into the picture, although very modestly, because of its belonging to the British Empire and as a result of the work of Western Orientalism and archaeology. The enormous importance of Buddhism as part of the history and ancient glory of India began to dawn thereby upon the minds of Western-educated Indians. Not as Hindus, but as nationalist Hindus, they began to realize Buddhism's significance as a national cultural asset, and consequently dropped the age-old idea about Buddhism as an non-Hindu heresy. Many able Indian philosophers, versed as well in Indian as in Western philosophy, aided by the efforts and results of

VI

When it comes to the relationship of the empirical world to the reality that lies beyond it or underlies it, which has been the main theme of this presentation up to this point—the word most often used in the context of describing it is 'māyā'. Modern Hinduism has expended much time and energy in clarifying this concept, as it had been widely misunderstood in the anterior period, resulting in the expression *māyāvādin* or a believer in the doctrine of māyā, when the word is understood as indicating the illusoriness of the world. The conflation of māyā with illusionism, like that of karma with fatalism, has been the bane of Hinduism that modern Hinduism has done much to counter. The problem of māyā is compounded by its criticism that it is Buddhism under the guise of Vedānta, and by the early Western criticism that it is a world-negating doctrine. Actually 'no theory has ever asserted that life is a dream and all experienced events are illusions. One or two later followers of Śaṁkara lend countenance to this hypothesis, but it cannot be regarded as representing the main tendency of Hindu thought.'[52] Nor is it 'proper language for *all* men to speak of the world as māyā (illusion)'[53] for then it leads to the following chain of reasoning:

If the individual soul and the world are unreal, then it may be argued by one who does not subscribe to the doctrine of Māyā as against those who hold it that you are teaching that an unreal soul has to escape from an unreal *Saṁsāra* and secure what you call mokṣa by means which are themselves unreal (such as Upaniṣad study) and that therefore mokṣa

Western scholarship, did (and do) not only share in the new attitude of spiritual and cultural self-affirmation, but claimed (and claim) the Buddha as a true son of India, trying to give him his place within the wide circle of Indian religio-philosophical thinking and metaphysical mysticism.'

[52] Radhakrishnan, S., *The Hindu View of Life,* London: George Allen & Unwin, 1927, p. 70.

[53] Kane, P.V., *History of Dharmaśāstra,* Vol. V, Part II, Poona: Bhandarkar Oriental Research Institute, 1962, p. 1509, emphasis added; also see David Godman, *The Teachings of Ramana Maharshi,* pp. 181–3.

itself is unreal. How the one Reality becomes many and expresses itself in the ever-changing physical world is really an inexplicable mystery, but that does not entitle all of us to say that the world is unreal or a dream. The few highly philosophical men may say that what is real is the one Absolute, that all else is only an appearances of that Absolute. Common men may, however, complain that explanations offered by these philosophers do not satisfy them or are beyond them.[54]

This is the dominant note struck in modern Hinduism and it represents a position in support of which several arguments can be adduced: (1) Not all schools of Hindu thought subscribe to the doctrine of māyā; (2) Those that ascribe to it understand it differently; (3) The view that according to the doctrine of māyā the world is an illusion is associated with Advaita Vedānta and 'is one of the most misunderstood elements of Vedānta'. The misunderstanding can be cleared if it is realized that 'there is the physical world with its manifold distinctions, but it must rest on something else; that something is called the *absolute brahman*. The relation between the

[54] *Ibid.*, p. 1509. P.V. Kane explains (pp. 1508–9): 'The highest metaphysical standpoint can be realized by only a few. For millions of men, the empirical standpoint alone remains and it is for them that texts speak of a personal God, ritual and sacrifices; they are only on the first rung of the ladder to enlightenment and are only dimly aware of God; there is a much smaller class of people other than the preceding, who pray, seek God and come to realize that God is both immanent and transcendent; there is a third class of a very few people, the great sages and masters, the spiritual elite such as Śaṅkarācārya, who reach the peak of pure monism, who lose the sense of the ego and who are ripe for entering into union with the One and they cannot and should not say that the individual soul and the physical world are all unreal (or Māyā). Both Bādarāyaṇa (V. S. II. 2. 29 "*Vaidharmyāc-ca na svapnādivat*") and Śaṅkarācārya are agreed that the ordinary physical world is entirely different from dreams and that the impressions in the waking state are not independent of existing objects. Apart from the question whether the word "Māyā" used in V. S. III. 2. 3 (Māyāmātram tu &c.) is used by Bādarāyaṇa in the sense in which Śaṅkarācārya understands it, it cannot be denied that Upaniṣad passages like Kaṭha Up. II. 4. 2, Praśna I. 16, Chān. Up. VIII. 3. 1–2, the prayer in Bṛ. Up. I. 3. 28 (*asato mā sadgamaya* &c.) could easily suggest the doctrine of Māyā and lead to it as an intelligible development. Hence the proper language for almost all men is not to speak about the world as "Māyā" (illusion).'

two is inexplicable and therefore it is spoken of as māyā;'[55] (4) If anything, Śaṅkara is an agnostic rather than an illusionist.[56] The arguments could be extended.[57]

It is wrong to say therefore that according to the doctrine of māyā the world is an illusion; it is equally wrong to hold that the world is ultimately real. In saying that the world is māyā, modern Hinduism is saying 'that there is something tricky about it. The trick lies in the way the world's materiality and multiplicity pass themselves off as being ultimately real—real apart from the stance from which we see them...'[58] And if we fall for this trick we, the *jīvas*, fall into *saṁsāra*.

The concept of the jīva in modern Hinduism does not differ radically from that in classical Hinduism. There is, however, a tendency to pass over the role of the *kāraṇa śarīra* or causal body, the third of the three constituents of the human personality—largely because its role is inconspicuous compared to that of the subtle body[59] (*sūkṣma śarīra*), which actually transmigrates from one gross (*sthūla*) body at the time of death to another. There is a stronger tendency to look upon the human personality as a psycho-physical organism, as *nāma rūpa*: 'A composite of physical and mental traits'.[60] That there is transmigration is generally accepted; who really transmigrates is a metaphysical issue. The point of emphasis in modern Hinduism is the distinction between the jīva and the *ātman*, and not so much the distinctions within the constituents of the jīva.

[55] *Ibid.*, p. 1510. But see M. Hiriyanna, *The Essentials of Indian Philosophy*, London: George Allen & Unvwin, 1949, p. 161.

[56] Radhakrishnan, S., *The Hindu View of Life*, p. 69.

[57] See *ibid.*, p. 65; M. Hiriyanna, *Outlines of Indian Philosophy*, London: George Allen & Unwin, 1932, p. 351; S. Radhakrishnan, *The Brahma Sūtra: The Philosophy of Spiritual Life*, London: George Allen & Unwin, 1960, pp. 137–40.

[58] Smith, Huston, *The World's Religions*, San Francisco: Harper, 1991, p. 70.

[59] Osborne, Arthur (ed.), *The Teachings of Bhagavan Sri Raman Maharshi in His Own Words*, p. 30.

[60] Radhakrishnan S. (tr.), *The Brahma Sūtra: The Philosophy of Spiritual Life*, p. 144.

We are the jīvas. 'The problem for philosophy is, why is there a world at all? And what are we all doing in it? Before we are able to answer these questions, we must know the nature of the world.... Each state is determined by what went before it. The world process has a pattern and a goal.'[61] This leads us naturally towards a consideration of the place of saṁsāra, karma, and *mokṣa* in modern Hinduism.

It is an interesting feature of modern Hinduism that although it has not abandoned the concepts of saṁsāra, karma, and mokṣa, it has re-examined them and, to a certain extent, tried to rationalize them. Reincarnation in animal life-forms is considered normal in classical Hinduism. The suggestion has been made in modern Hinduism that 'when it is said that the human soul suffers the indignity of animal life, the suggestion is figurative, not literal. It means that it is reborn in an irrational existence comparable to animal life and not that it is actually attached to the body of an animal.'[62] Mahatma Gandhi imparts to it an almost opposite figural interpretation: 'It is my implicit belief that snakes, tigers, etc., are God's answer to the poisonous wicked evil thoughts that we harbour. Anna Kingsford saw in the streets of Paris tigers in men already taking shape. I believe that all life is one. Thoughts take definite forms.'[63] Moreover, even the idea of rebirth has been questioned, not in the sense that it might not occur, but in the sense that as the crucial issue is what makes it recur, we should forget about past or future lives and zero in on this one—for ultimately saṁsāra is the flow of thoughts, etc., spilling over from one life to another. So if mokṣa is to be attained, this flow must be stopped, which is rooted in the ego. Hence, even the question of types of mokṣa becomes somewhat redundant. Thus, Ramaṇa Maharṣi propounded: 'If it is said that liberation is of three kinds, with form, or without form, or with or without form, then let me tell you [that] the extinction of the ego that asks which form of Liberation

[61] *Ibid.*, p. 136.
[62] *Ibid.*, p. 204.
[63] M.K. Gandhi, *Hindu Dharma*, p. 190.

is true is the only true Liberation.'[64] It is the ego which generates karma and, in some forms of modern Hinduism, this ego or the I-thought is similarly made short work of. Ramaṇa Maharṣi, again:

You must distinguish between the 'I', pure in itself, and the 'I'-thought. The latter, being merely a thought, sees subject and object, sleeps, wakes up, eats and thinks, dies and is reborn. But the pure 'I' is the pure being, eternal existence, free from ignorance and thought-illusion. If you stay as the 'I', your being alone, without thought, the 'I'-thought will disappear and the delusion will vanish for ever.[65]

This paves the way for a discussion of the paths of liberation, or the various yogas. The technique of erasing the ego described above belongs to *jñāna-yoga*, or the path of knowledge. The same result is achieved on the path of devotion, or *bhakti-yoga*, by surrendering the ego to God and on the path of action, or *karma yoga*, by performing actions without the sense of doership. The concept of karma itself has been recontextualized in modern Hinduism, under the influence of the doctrine of karma yoga within it, as indicating both a greater measure of activism and also a greater measure of ameliorative activism. In the context of modern Hinduism, Hindu

leaders are not ashamed to point out how remiss we have been in the matter of social service, how wrong we have been in interpreting the Law of karma, so as to provide ourselves with a cloak for covering our neglect of our duties to our neighbours and our indifference to the cries of the poor and the down-trodden. They are never tired of pointing out how slow we are when compared with the followers of other religions in working for social amelioration, in spite of our boasted spirituality. Swami Vivekananda, Tagore and Gandhi were never tired of pointing out that spirituality does not consist in turning our back on poverty, ignorance and misery in the world in a vain attempt to save our souls, but that it consists in fully facing them and fighting against them till they are vanquished. There is no doubt that, as a result of their teaching, a large fund of religious feeling has been released for social work in the country. Thousands of men and women are today working in a

[64] Osborne, Arthur (ed.), *The Teachings of Bhagavan Sri Raman Maharshi in His Own Words,* p. 253.

[65] Godman, David (ed.), *The Teachings of Sri Ramana Maharshi,* p. 52.

religious spirit not only in the Ramakrishna Mission, but also in the various fields of social service—temperance, promotion of handspinning and weaving and other village industries and Harijan uplift—inaugurated by Mahatma Gandhi. Such a thing was practically unknown before this Renaissance.[66]

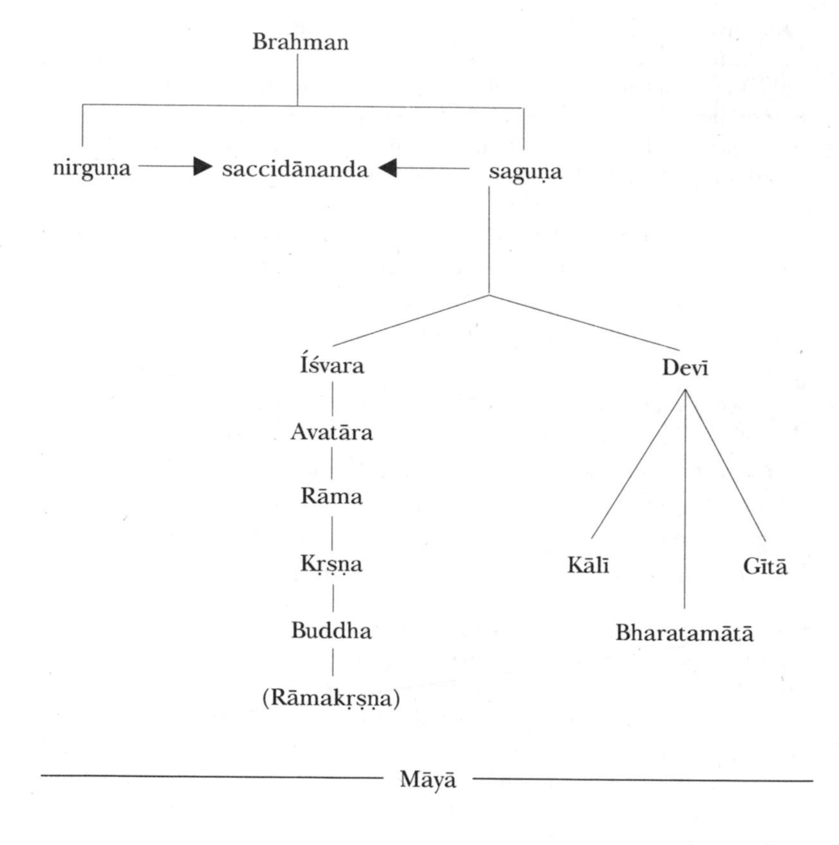

VII

The developments of modern Hindu thought arc far more striking in the socio-ethical, as compared to the metaphysical, dimension for it is in the realm of social thought that modern Hinduism has made its most significant contributions. The

[66] Sarma, D.S., *Hinduism Through the Ages*, pp. 264–5.

very fact that this point in this essay constitutes a natural divide provides the necessary evidence of what the section is itself going to claim. Pre-modern Hinduism regarded itself as a seamless web, so that 'to many Hindus themselves, it was an eyeopener in this period to be taught that what really matters in religion is its philosophy based on religious experience, and not the particular social arrangements or beliefs in particular deities in which it embodied itself in the past.' D.S. Sarma goes on to add: 'To know that the soul of a religion is different from its body, that the former is imperishable, while the latter is perishable, and that our myths and rites and castes belong to the latter and not the former is a great education in itself, and it has made the path of social reform easy.'[67] In fact, this distinguishing the inessential from the essential is one of the essentials of modern Hindu thought, and it may have succeeded in this direction more than it needed to. Nothing succeeds like excess. As R. Boyd points out: 'For the modern educated man in India religion is philosophy or it is nothing.'[68]

This is of course an overstatement, but points in the right direction. It is an overstatement because the reform—the social reform of Hinduism that consistently maintains a lofty philosophical platform—is an essential aspect of modern Hinduism. Several factors point in this direction: (1) There was a comprehensive questioning of the Hindu world-view prompted by the impact of modernity under whose influence image-worship and the doctrine of reincarnation came under fierce theological attack, along with a critique of its social evils. This attack, though it did make a dent, failed to dislodge these theological elements, but the social critique of Hinduism has both been widely accepted and has also proved essentially effective;[69] (2) The impact of the Western presence in India

[67] Sarma, D.S., *Hinduism Through the Ages*, p. 262.

[68] Boyd, R. *An Introduction to Indian Christian Theology*, Madras: Christian Literature Society, 1979, p. 262.

[69] See K.M. Panikkar, *Hindu Society at the Cross Roads*, Bombay: Asia Publishing House, 1961, passim.

was felt most keenly in this area, as also the activity of the Christian missions;[70] (3) Almost every major Hindu religious figure of modern Hinduism turned his attention to the condition of the lower classes and attacked untouchability;[71] and (4) The Hindu Renaissance may itself be said to have 'started with social reform. It started with Ram Mohun Roy's agitation for the abolition of Sati. The chief objective of the Brahmo Samaj and the Prarthana Samaj was social reform, and when it was achieved they lost their momentum to a large extent.'[72] The following statement of D.S. Sarma virtues clinches the issue:

> To understand the achievements of the present Renaissance in the field of social reform, we have only to compare the state of Hindu society today with what it was before this movement began. Today Sati has become an incredible thing of the past. Child-marriages and polygamy have become illegal. Widow-marriages have been made possible. Provision is made for divorce. Foreign travel has become very common. The ban against inter-dining has been lifted. The caste system has become less rigid. And, thanks to Mahatma Gandhi, the demon of untouchability has been overthrown. Women have become educated and have begun to occupy the highest offices in the State. Of course, all that has been done so far is very little compared with what has yet to be done, especially in the way of communal unity. We are as yet only at the beginning of things. But in every direction the ice has been broken, and water has begun to flow. Further progress is only a matter of time. Hereafter, there can be no going back to the evil customs and the harmful restrictions of our ages of decadence. The pace of events has hitherto been slow all over the world. But in future the pace is bound to be much more rapid, as a result of the radio, the aeroplane, the motor-bus, and other mechanical inventions of the age. We hope that Hindu society will hereafter march more rapidly to its destined goal with the strength it has derived from the movement for social reform during this period.[73]

[70] Basham, A.L., 'Hinduism', in *The Concise Encyclopedia of Living Faiths*, R.C. Zaehner (ed.), Boston: Beacon Press, 1967, p. 256.

[71] Sharma, Arvind, *Modern Hindu Thought: The Essential Texts*, New Delhi: Oxford University Press, 2002, *passim*.

[72] Sarma, D.S., *Hinduism Through the Ages*, pp. 262–3.

[73] *Ibid.*, p. 263.

VIII

The crucial point to consider now is how modern Hinduism was able to bring about such a change, to the extent it did, within the umbrella or under the banner of Hinduism itself.

This point is no better illustrated than by the case of the caste system. This whole period witnessed an attack on the caste system, ever since Rammohun Roy drew attention to it as a fatal flaw of Hinduism. It was subject to attack thus both from the inside as well as the outside—for, the external critics of Hinduism were as quick to identify this fault-line within it as the internal critics. Hendrik Kraemer makes the interesting observation that 'It was caste that provided for Hinduism the impregnable shell of defence against the shock of Muslim invasion. At the historical moment considered here, the Western invasion by its quite different nature made caste instead of a *defence*, a moral and social *offence*.'[74]

It would be tedious to trace the history of this attack on the caste system, but the manner in which it impinged on the self-awareness of modern Hinduism may be illustrated with the help of an example. The role of Advaita Vedānta in the context of modern Hinduism is manifold, but two facets of it may be highlighted here. *Externally*, it was used to project Hindu philosophical superiority[75], while *internally* it was reworked to revalorize the universe ontologically.[76] There is an anecdote about the life of its most famous formulator, Śaṅkara (ninth century), in which he is depicted as encountering an untouchable in a narrow street in Benares.[77] As is well known, a fundamental tenet of the Advaita Vedānta is non-dualism (advaita). So, when Śaṅkara asked the untouchable to move out of his way, the latter reproached him tactfully on the

[74] See Hendrik Kraemer, *World Cultures and World Religions: The Coming Dialogue*, London: Lutterworth Press, 1960, p. 131 note 2.

[75] *Ibid.*, p. 152 ff.

[76] Radhakrishnan, S., *The Hindu View of Life*, New York: The Macmillan Company, 1927, pp. 47–9.

[77] Pande, Govindra Chandra, *Life and Thought of Śaṅkarācārya*, Delhi: Motilal Banarsidass, 1994, p. 87.

inconsistency between his creed and conduct. The untouchable later revealed himself as Śiva and the four leashed dogs as the four Vedas.

The perception of this contradiction between the intellectual espousal to the untouchable brahman and the simultaneous practice of untouchability as a social reality reveals the raw nerve of even classical Hinduism on this touchy point. Apart from its inherently remarkable nature, the way the account has been mined in modern Hinduism is even more remarkable. It is constantly used in modern Hinduism to philosophically delegitimize caste distinctions.[78] One example must suffice. S. Radhakrishnan writes:

> There is a story that when Śaṅkara, in spite of his non-dualism asked an outcaste to clear the way for him, the outcaste who was God himself asked: 'Do you wish my body to leave your body or my spirit to leave your spirit?' If democracy is to be seriously implemented, then caste and untouchability should go.[79]

The abruptness of the pronouncement that caste and untouchability must go actually conceals the gradual movement within Hinduism in this direction, and in the thinking of Radhakrishnan himself, in particular. In his famous *Hindu View of Life*, for example, Radhakrishnan proleptically attributes the evils of the caste system to its degeneration, and goes on to say: 'It is not my purpose this evening to relate the evils of the system; I wish to draw your attention to the underlying principles.'[80] He then proceeds to delineate the system from an ideal plane. In this ideal version, equality replaces hierarchy; harmony replaces antagonism; and worth replaces birth. That *varṇa* is determined by action (karma) and not birth (*janma*) is a chorus that rises to a crescendo[81] but ends up like a Gregorian chant that does not transform the life of the parishioners once they leave the church, howsoever lofty it

[78] M.K. Gandhi, *Hindu Dharma*, p. 21; etc.

[79] Radhakrishnan S. (tr.), *The Brahma Sūtra: The Philosophy of Spiritual Life*, pp. 162–3.

[80] *Ibid.*, p. 93.

[81] Kane, P.V., *History of Dharmaśāstra*, Vol. V, Part II, p. 1632 ff, especially, pp. 1642–3.

sounds. So, in the end, one asks for the dissolution of the system itself.[82]

An important distinction must be made between the caste system as such, and *discrimination* based on caste, in discussing the caste system in modern Hinduism—just as a distinction between caste as varṇa and caste as *jāti* needs to be made in a discussion of it in classical Hinduism. It is quite clear that the trend in modern Hinduism is irreversibly towards the elimination of discrimination based on caste; in fact, affirmative action recently undertaken in India is even suggestive of steps to compensate for past discrimination on this account. However, while discrimination based on caste can be abolished, can the caste system be abolished? Discrimination based on race (i.e., racism) can be abolished, but can races be abolished? Perhaps, in both cases, intermarriages over the long run can achieve this goal; the more immediate aim should be to abolish discrimination based on them. The thrust of modern Hinduism certainly lies in that direction.

In view of this thrust, it is surprising that most exponents of modern Hinduism have overlooked an account of the genesis of the caste system that is almost as ancient as the one found in the *Puruṣasūkta*, but which offers a very different version of the origin of the caste system. According to the *Puruṣasūkta* version, all the varṇas arose more or less simultaneously out of the dismemberment of a macranthropus in a primeval sacrifice.[83] According to this alternative account, found in the *Śatapatha Brāhmaṇa*,[84] and then in the *Bṛhadāraṇyaka Upaniṣad*,[85] in the beginning there was only one varṇa, and the other varṇas arose after it in succession and in many versions. This account is much more in keeping with modern sentiments on the issue, and is incorporated in the diagram that follows.

[82] Harris, Ishwar C., *Radhakrishnan: Profile of a Universalist*, Calcutta: Minerva Associates [Publications] Pvt. Ltd., 1982, Preface.

[83] Basham, A.L., *The Wonder That Was India*, New Delhi: Rupa & Co., 1999 [1954], pp. 240–1.

[84] Muir, J., *Original Sanskrit Texts*, Vol. I, Delhi: Oriental Publishers, 1972, pp. 19–20.

[85] Radhakrishnan S. (ed.), *The Principal Upaniṣads*, Atlantic Highlands, N.J.: Humanities Press International, 1992 [1953], pp. 169–71.

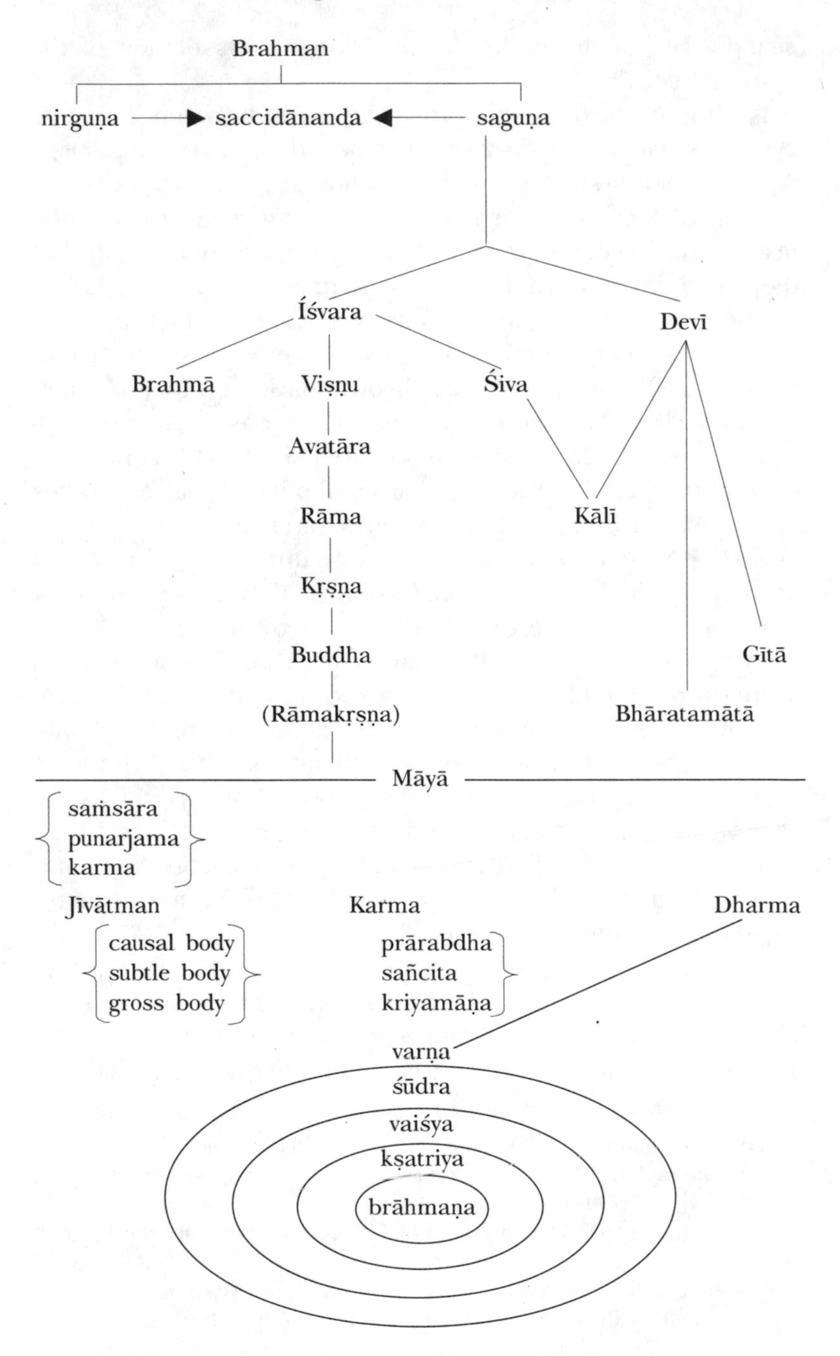
Brahman
nirguṇa
saccidānanda
saguṇa
Íśvara
Devī
Brahmā
Viṣṇu
Śiva
Avatāra
Rāma
Kālī
Kṛṣṇa
Buddha
Gītā
(Rāmakṛṣṇa)
Bhāratamātā
Māyā
saṁsāra
punarjama
karma
Jīvātman
Karma
Dharma
causal body
subtle body
gross body
prārabdha
sañcita
kriyamāṇa
varṇa
śūdra
vaiśya
kṣatriya
brāhmaṇa

IX

While the caste system has been roundly criticized, its allied doctrine, the *āśrama* system—or the system of the stages of life—has received praise.[86] Although it is tempting to believe that, as the normal life-span was taken to be a hundred years, each stage of life would be meant to cover twenty-five years—and an idealized vision would perhaps conform to this. However, 'as no one could say how long one might live, it is not to be supposed that each stage was of 25 years; all that is meant is that a man may, if he lives long, pass through the four stages,'[87] namely, those of (1) the celibate student (*brahmacarya*); (2) the householder (*gṛhastha*); (3) the hermit (*vānaprastha*); and (4) the renunciate (*sannyāsa*).

Two points need to be noted with regard to the āśrama system in modern Hinduism. Both spring from the fact that this scheme represents an attempt to harmonize the two opposing tendencies of first, engagement in worldly duties and second, renunciation of worldly duties, respectively known as *pravṛtti* and *nivṛtti*. It will be recalled that Arjuna, on the eve of the Mahābhārata war, and Yudhiṣṭhira after it, felt a strong inclination to renounce the world, a course from which they were successfully dissuaded. It could be argued that the Bhagavadgītā, especially in view of its popularity, resolves the issue without resorting to the doctrine of the stages of life by establishing the case of nivṛtti in pravṛtti, or renunciation in action rather than renunciation of action. Some observers of modern Hinduism feel, however, that although the '*Gita*'s solution is brilliant',[88] it is not feasible for many, who perhaps 'find it difficult to live in the world while remaining detached from it' and continue to feel the tension between the two orientations. In other words, the doctrine of karmayoga, while easy to accept in theory, may be difficult to apply in practice. This then leads to the second point that probably,

[86] Kane, P.V., *History of Dharmaśāstra*, Vol. V, Part II, p. 1646.

[87] *Ibid.*, p. 1644.

[88] Kinsley, David R. *Hinduism: A Cultural Perspective* (second edition), Englewod Cliffs, New Jersey: Prentice Hall, 1982, p. 38.

The solutions presented in the *Mahabharata* to Arjuna's and Yudhishthira's dilemmas never dissolved the tension between the paths of dharma and renunciation. To this day the tension persists, and for many Hindus the two paths are seen as very different religious possibilities. The solution of the Law Books—namely, the four stages of life, in which renunciation is postponed until old age—is usually ignored. Most world renouncers in India leave the world while still young. Most famous Indian saints who renounced the world did so well before they had fulfilled their social obligations. On the other hand, the vast majority of Hindus who do not renounce the world as youths never renounce the world, preferring to remain in society during their old age.[89]

The Bhagavadgītā nevertheless seems to offer a fairly persuasive reconciliation at the intellectual level, so that the modern Hindu does not confront massive cognitive dissonance in the context of the āśrama system in the modern world.

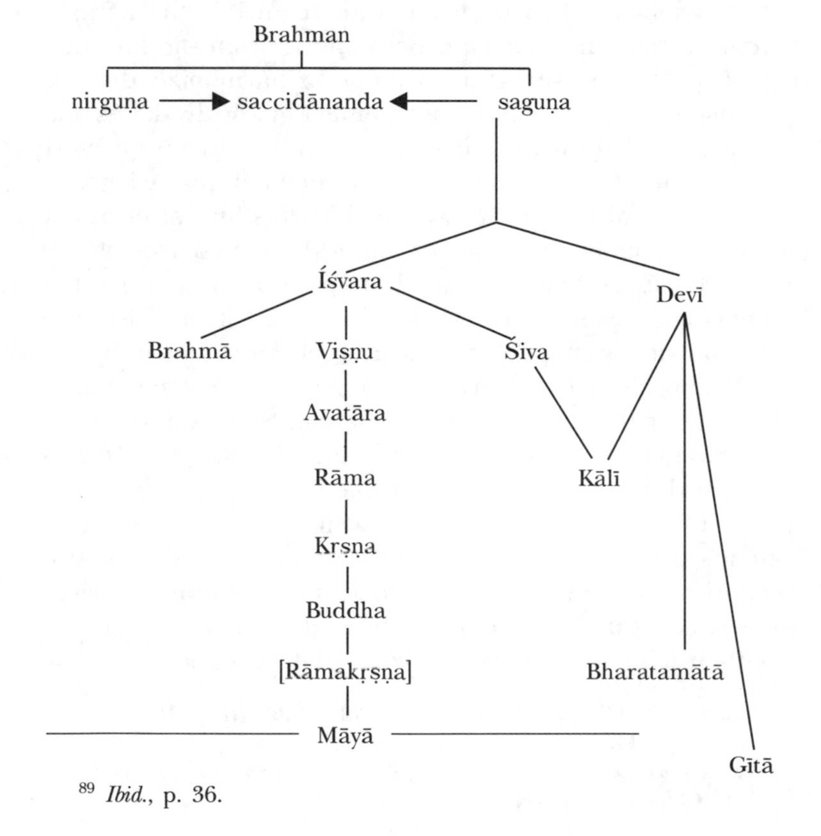

[89] *Ibid.*, p. 36.

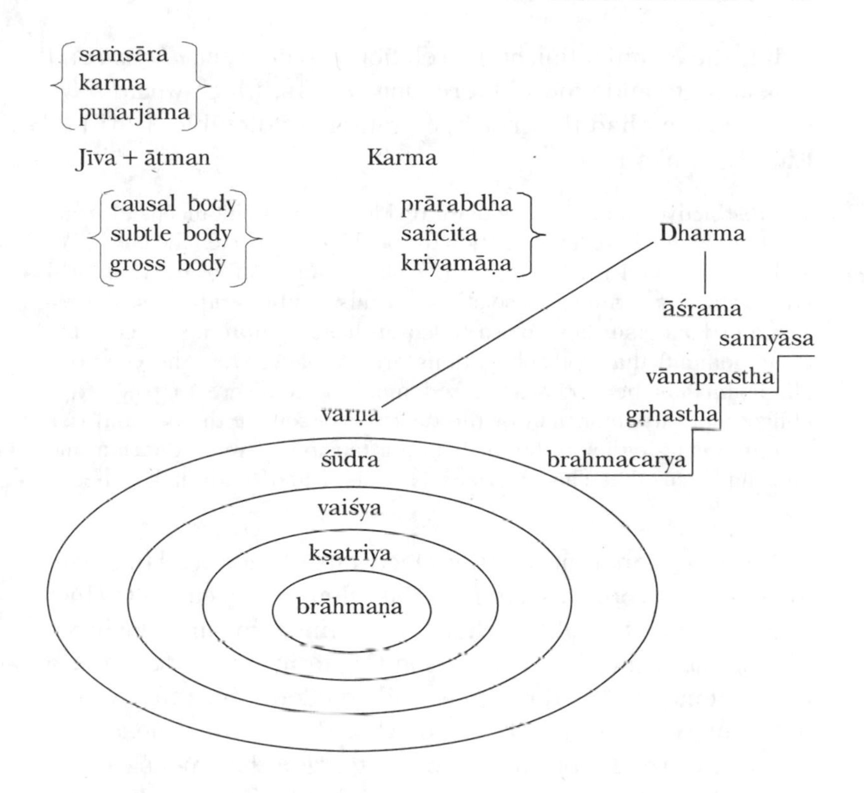

X

The various stages of life are also connected with the various goals of life, as embodied in the doctrine of the *puruṣārthas.* One may begin by observing that *artha* (wealth) and *kāma* (pleasures) are now fully recognized in their own right with the perhaps greater recognition of this-worldliness in philosophical Hinduism in modern times, as compared to some other phases of its history. Some Hindus now express alarm at the inroads that consumerism and hedonism are making, not only in society but also in terms of social norms. However, as India gradually moves towards enjoying a higher standard of living than was possible in colonial times, some axiological adjustment is inevitable.

It is the examination of the relationship between *dharma* and mokṣa that yields more interesting results, which would have been exciting had they not been rather predictable. David R. Kinsley thinks that

The distinctive nature of Hinduism resides in its simultaneous affirmation that people have an obligation to uphold the world, on the one hand, and to transcend the world, on the other hand. Although traditional Hinduism has formulated solutions to this double emphasis, the essence of Hinduism lies not so much in these compromises as in the clear demand that both obligations are absolute. Over the centuries Hinduism has been characterized more by a desire to push each obligation to its limit than by the desire to reconcile the two and risk compromising either of them. It is the tension between dharma and moksha, then, that characterizes Hinduism and lends it its special appeal.[90]

It seems apparent that the electricity of modern Hinduism also comes from this charge, this alternating current. However, the point could perhaps be refined by introducing a distinction drawn by Troy Wilson Organ in relation to mokṣa or freedom as 'freedom *from* and freedom *for*, release and opportunity.'[91] On the basis of this distinction 'those who stress the freedom-from component argue that mokṣa is the removal of constraints, keeping hands off, leaving alone, relaxing of controls,' while those who 'stress the freedom for component argue that mokṣa is the opportunity and ability to actualize inherent potentialities'.[92] If, in classical Hinduism, mokṣa was primarily oriented toward the first understanding, in modern Hinduism the orientation seems to lie as much toward the other.

* * *

The chapters that follow will take up the key concepts introduced to offer a more detailed and elaborate analysis of

[90] Kinsley, David R., *Hinduism: A Cultural Perspective*, p. 176.

[91] Organ, Troy Wilson, *Hinduism: Its Historical Development*, Woodbury, New York: Barron's Educational Series, Inc., 1974, p. 202.

[92] *Ibid.*

each. The reader would have noticed, for instance, that in the evolving diagrams that depict the constellation of these key concepts, three types of karma—*prārabdha, sañcita, kriyamāṇa*—are introduced but not commented upon in the general introduction. Such a detailed explanation will now be available in the chapter on karma. The same applies for other concepts.

These explanatory chapters move progressively down the chart, elaborating each term broadly in the order in which it appears.

PART THREE
Terms and Tenets

III

Brahman
Nirguṇa and Saguṇa

Advaita Vedānta has been a strong force in modern Hinduism, and it has been estimated that three-fourths of modern Hindu intellectuals subscribe to it. It may also be noted that 'the more important spokesmen of the reawakening or Renaissance experienced by Hinduism from about the middle of the nineteenth century onwards were closer to Advaita Vedānta in their metaphysical outlook. Ramakrishna Paramhamsa (1836–86) and his illustrious disciple Vivekananda (1863–1902) were both Advaitins by conviction, and even Mahatma Gandhi, who was at once a Karmayogin and a believer in bhakti, was an Advaitin in his metaphysical faith.' It may be further added that 'this is also true of the more influential pre-Independence scholars such as Lokmanya Tilak and Dr Radhakrishnan.'[1] While there are elements of exaggeration in these statements, there can be little doubt that modern Hinduism has primarily projected Advaita Vedānta in its confrontation with the West as its religious philosophy, which has evolved past the monotheism of the West and surpassed it with monism.[2]

[1] Devaraja, N.K., *op. cit.*, p. 64.

[2] But see Troy Wilson Organ, *op. cit.*, p. 7.

However, modern Advaitins, though inspired by Śaṅkara, only follow his system in a general outline rather than in detail. This is true of even such a well-known exponent of Advaita Vedānta as S. Radhakrishnan.[3] Many modern thinkers have chosen to utilize the categories of thought that make up the system of Advaita, rather than the system of Advaita itself, so that in the end they have come up with their own systems, or quasi-systems, using various categories of Advaita. This seems to be a major reason why so many of them are called Advaitic—or at times appear Advaitic.

There is, however, a definite tendency to move away from nirguṇa brahman as a mere blank, or the appearance that it might be so. One way of dispelling such a mistaken impression would be to use the word *guṇa* not in the general sense of quality, but as relating to the three guṇas of *sattva, rajas,* and *tamas.* In that case, brahman, as nirguṇa, is beyond them, while Íśvara or saguṇa brahman could be depicted as 'hidden in his own guṇas' (*Śvetāśvatara Upaniṣad* I.3). The three guṇas could then correspond to the three gods of the *trimūrti.*[4] *Prakṛti* then could take the place assigned to *Devī* in the chart.

[3] Murty, K. Satchidananda and Ashok Vohra, *Radhakrishnana: His Life and Ideas,* Delhi: Ajanta Publications, 1989, p. 211.

[4] An invocatory verse at the beginning of Bāṇa's *Kādambarī* makes this point felicitously.

IV

Íśvara

Íśvara has received great emphasis in modern Hinduism—but in a non-sectarian manner. Historians of Hindu religion have noted that, in classical Hinduism, the identification of Íśvara with one of the three members of the trimūrti—Brāhmā, Viṣṇu, or Śiva, was extremely strong. There is a tendency in modern Hinduism to think of God in more abstract terms. The poems of Rabindranath Tagore provide a relevant illustration of this point. D. S. Sarma notes that Tagore 'dispenses with all mythological symbols and sectarian names and forms. He uses the universal language of man. He speaks of God as king, master, friend, father, poet, bridegroom, or lover, and not as any mythological deity or avatār.'[5] This trend characterizes modern Hindu thought. Although Dayānanda Sarasvatī (1824–83) was born in a Śaiva family, he spoke of God in general, and not as Śiva. This tendency was also abetted by Advaita Vedānta in its own way, for that is what Rāmakṛṣṇa obviously meant when he said: 'According to the Vedānta, there is no Incarnation of God. The Vedāntists say that Rāma and Krishna are but two waves in the Ocean of Satchidānanda.'[6]

[5] Sarma, D.S., *Studies in the Renaissance of Hinduism*, Benaras: Benaras Hindu University, 1944, p. 388.

[6] Swami Nikhilananda, *The Gospel of Sri Ramakrishna*, p. 306.

Thus, three of the major associations of theism in classical Hinduism—(1) image-worship, (2) sectarianism, and (3) belief in incarnation—seemed at one point ready to fall by the wayside in modern Hinduism. On the whole, however, this did not happen.[7] Image-worship continues virtually unaffected, and the doctrine of incarnation has been extended to include non-Hindu figures such as Jesus Christ,[8]—it has gained a certain vogue in Śaiva theology, which is traditionally less characterized by a doctrine of incarnation compared to the Vaiṣṇava. The modern God-man, Sathya Sai Baba, for instance, is regarded as an incarnation of Śiva.[9]

Sectarianism, on the other hand, has suffered a marked decline, although it has not disappeared. Ishwar C. Harris notes:

> It is not true that there are no sectarian conflicts within Hinduism. Even Śaṅkara is said to have mediated between Vaiṣṇavites and Śaivites when he created the image of *'Badrivishal'* which is enshrined at the great temple of Badrinath in North India. The image is supposed to represent a unity between Śiva and Viṣṇu. Consequently, harmony is expected between the followers of these two deities. I might add that often emotions are high when a community is faced with the decision of which deity to enshrine in a newly built temple in India. Now these disputes can be dismissed as isolated incidents if one chooses to do so. It is true that many temples will represent other deities and even build shrines for them within the temple courtyard, even though the main shrine is dedicated to a particular god like Śiva or Viṣṇu.[10]

In the context of modern Hinduism, the concept of the trimūrti may then be replaced by another: the triple description of brahman as sat, cit, and ānanda, or saccidānanda brahman. The first point to note here is that while the trimūrti could only be applied to Íśvara or saguṇa brahma and not to

[7] Kraemer, Hendrik, *World Cultures and World Religions: The Coming Dialogue*, p. 155.

[8] Sen, K.M., *Hinduism*, p. 73.

[9] Murphet, Howard, *Sai Baba Avatar*, Delhi: Macmillan, 1978, *passim.*

[10] Harris, Ishwar C., *Radhakrishnan: The Profile of a Universalist*, Calcutta: Minerva Associates [Publication] Pvt. Ltd., 1982, p. 225.

nirguṇa brahma, the appellation saccidānanda can be applied to both, but is explained somewhat differently.

One way in which this appellation operates in modern Hinduism, when applied to nirguṇa brahma is as follows:

The spiritual and unitary character of this absolute reality is very well expressed by the classical phrase *saccidānanda*. As a single term defining its nature, it is met with only in the later Upanishads; but its three elements—*sat*, *cit* and *ānanda*—are used of Brahman, singly and in pairs, even in the earliest of them. *Sat*, which means 'being,' points to the positive character of Brahman distinguishing it from all non-being. But positive entities, to judge from our experience, may be spiritual or not. The next epithet *cit*, which means 'sentience,' shows that it is spiritual. The last epithet *ānanda*, which stands for 'peace,' indicates its unitary and all-embracing character, inasmuch as variety is the source of all trouble and restlessness. 'Fear arises from the other,' as the famous Upanishadic saying has it. Thus the three epithets together signify that Brahman is the sole spiritual reality or the Absolute, which comprehends not only all being (*sat*) but also all thought (*cit*) so that whatever partakes of the character of either must eventually be traced to it.[11]

When applied to *saguṇa* brahma or Íśvara, it may be elaborated as follows.

The word *Satya* (Truth) is derived from *Sat*, which means 'being.' Nothing is or exists in reality except Truth. That is why *Sat* or Truth is perhaps the most important name of God. In fact it is more correct to say that Truth is God, than to say that God is Truth. But as we cannot do without a ruler or a general, names of God such as 'King of Kings' or 'the Almighty' are and will remain generally current. On deeper thinking, however, it will be realized, that *Sat* or *Satya* is the only correct and fully significant name for God.

And where there is Truth, there also is knowledge which is true. Where there is no Truth, there can be no true knowledge. That is why the word *Chit* or knowledge is associated with the name of God. And where there is true knowledge, there is always bliss (*Ananda*). There sorrow has no place. And even as Truth is eternal, so is the bliss derived from it. Hence we know God as *Sat-chit-ananda*, One who combines in Himself Truth, Knowledge and Bliss.[12]

[11] Hiriyanna, M., *The Essentials of Indian Philosophy*, p. 22.

[12] M.K. Gandhi, *Hindu Dharma*, p. 221. This passage was also cited earlier.

Rāmakṛṣṇa even uses saccidānanda as a synonym of brahman itself, both saguṇa and nirguṇa, as when he says:

The Truth established in the Vedas, the Purānas, and the Tantras is but one Satchidānanda. In the Vedas It is called Brahman, in the Purānas It is called Krishna, Rāma, and so on, and in the Tantras It is called Śiva. The one Satchidānanda is called Brahman, Krishna, and Śiva.[13]

[13] Swami Nikhilananda (tr.), *The Gospel of Sri Ramakrishṇa*, p. 265. Also see p. 490.

V

Devī

The depiction of the ultimate reality as a feminine principle or devī serves to immediately draw attention to the Goddess tradition and its role in modern Hinduism. Various manifestations of this as Kālī the Mother, Mother India, Mother Religion, Mother Gītā have been alluded to earlier. It is perhaps significant that even Nirad Chaudhuri, a writer otherwise critical of Hinduism, talks in a very different vein when he talks of Kālī.[14] So the obvious point to make is that the Goddess tradition, which puts her on par with God, is alive and well, to the extent that even the possibility of using it as a positive resource for other religious traditions has also been mooted.[15]

In terms of modern Hinduism, the role of the Devī in the feminist movement needs to be examined, especially as some reviews of a Tantrika text such as the *Mahānirvāṇa Tantra* in the last century described Tantrism itself as 'religious feminism gone mad' and described Tantra as 'the feminization of orthodox Vedanta...a doctrine of suffragette monists.'[16] Obviously, the reviewer said this in sharp criticism, not

[14] Chaudhuri, Nirad C., *Hinduism: A Religion to Live By*, New York: Oxford University Press, 1979, p. 246: '...the worshippers of Durga or Kali never considered them in any light except as a divine mother.'

[15] *Ibid.*, Part Three, Chapter II.

[16] I owe this information to Lowell Jaks.

realizing that less than a century later, the same description might come to be treated as an endearing compliment!

A point calls for its examination in the context of modern Hinduism: What role does the Goddess tradition actually play in the life of Indian men and women? Does the Goddess tradition serve as a positive resource for women, or is it merely a theological compensation for social subordination? These points need to be investigated as it has been claimed that 'a study of Hindu Goddess worship does not allow us, for instance, to predict with any certainty the relationship of women and men in Indian society.'[17]

An intriguing precedent is provided on the question of feminism and the Goddess by the metaphorical metamorphosis of the sacrifice of Kālī during the threshold years of the nationalist movement in Bengal, as described by Valentine Chirol:

> In 1906 I was visiting one of the Hindu temples at Benares and found in the courtyard a number of young students who had come on an excursion from Bengal. I got into conversation with them, and they soon began to air, for my benefit, their political views, which were decidedly 'advanced.' They were, however, quite civil and friendly, and they invited me to come up to the temple door and see them sacrifice to Kali a poor bleating kid that they had brought with them. When I declined, one of them who had already assumed a rather more truculent tone came forward and pressed me, saying that if I would accompany them they would not mind even sacrificing a white goat. There was a general shout of laughter at what was evidently regarded by the others as a huge joke. I turned away, though I did not then understand its grim humour, as I do now.[18]

The contemporary appropriation of the Devī is however proceeding less in a nationalist and more in a feminist context. As Klaus K. Klostermaier points out:

> Lately Western scholars have shown great interest in the various forms of Devī and her worship. This is partly due to the development of

[17] Preston, James J., 'Goddess Worship: Theoretical Perspectives', in *The Encyclopedia of Religion*, Mircea Eliade (ed.), Vol. 6, New York: Macmillan Publishing Company, 1987, p. 56.

[18] Chirol, Valentine, *Indian Unrest*, London: Macmillan & Co. 1910, p. 103. Also see pp. 345–6.

feminist perspectives also in religion. It is no longer uncommon for Westerners to speak of God as Mother rather than as Father and address her in terms not unlike the prayers Hindus have uttered for centuries to Devī. In addition, the importance of Devī in the practical political sphere of India has been highlighted.... The relation between Śakti and political power does not belong to the past alone. Several śāktas like Yogi Dhirendra Brahmacari were associated with top-ranking politicians of post-Independence India, and at one point a Tantrika priest was hired by members of an opposition party to perform a Tāntric ritual with a view to killing Prime Minster Indira Gandhi.[19]

It could be argued that the study of the Goddess is currently the centre of maximum interest in the study of Hinduism in the West,[20] and gaining increasing attention in India.

[19] Klostermaier, Klaus K., *op. cit.*, p. 293.

[20] See Elaine Craddock's Review of *At the Feet of the Goddess: The Divine Feminine in Local Hindu Religion*, Brighton and Portland, Oregon: Sussex Academic Press, 2002, by Lynn Foulston in *The Journal of Asian Studies* 63:1:222–3 (February 2004).

VI

Trimūrti

A doctrine of trinity has been described, in relation to classical Hinduism, as 'the most remarkable feature of classical Indian mythology' that provides for 'the coexistence, as part of a single visionary conception, to the three gods Brahmā, Vishnu, and Shiva. This trinity (in Sanskrit Trimūrti, "The Three Forms") does not appear as such until fairly late and does not quite become a separate object of worship,'[21] being affiliated, earlier, with one of the three figures themselves. In modern Hinduism, the doctrine of trimūrti tends to be associated with God as such, and is a convenient doctrine for relating God to the universe, as this universe undergoes the processes of manifestation, maintenance, and dissolution. The presence of the trinity in Christianity also tends to highlight this Hindu counterpart, while the doctrine of saccidānanda brahma, with its triple components of sat, cit, and ānanda, presents itself as yet another candidate for comparison.

Hindu metaphysical categories can, in fact, give rise to several trinities. If, to the division of Brahman as without attributes (nirguṇa) and with attributes (saguṇa), we add the description as beyond attributes (*para*) then a trinity in terms

[21] Renou, Louis, *The Nature of Hinduism*, Patrick Evans (tr), New York: Walker and Company, 1951, p. 42.

of Brahman can be identified. Saccidānanda, as a triple description of Brahman, has already been referred to. Then there is the trinity of the three 'male' gods which function in relation to not God, but Goddess (Devī) as the ultimate principle, when they are commissioned by her to perform their cosmic roles. Moreover, Íśvara and Devī can be paired, and the product of their union could constitute another trinity! This does not occur in theology, but does appear in mythology as when Śiva, of whom the word Íśvara is also a personal name, unites with Devī as Śakti.

In other words, along with a doctrine of trinity of classical origin analogous to the Christian, the categories of modern Hindu thought are capable of generating several trinities—even a trinity of trinities as it were, thus testifying Hinduism's penchant for expansion, classification, and even infinite or at least indefinite extension.

One such philosophical extension may be taken into particular account here. If one reverts momentarily to the consideration of Brahman as saccidānanda, one realizes that, according to Aurobindo Ghose, it represents the 'unknown, omnipresent, indispensable' which human consciousness, 'whether in knowledge or sentiment or in sensation and action', is eternally seeking. And, further, that Aurobindo's system itself involves two trinities, as it were: the higher one consisting of sat, cit, and ānanda, translated as Pure Existent, Consciousness-Force, and Delight of Existence, which with the Supermind constitute a quaternary, and a lower one consisting of Mind, Life, and Matter, being subordinate respectively to Supermind, cit, and sat. This constitutes the sevenfold chord of being.

VII

Brahmā

There is not much to say about Brahmā in the context of modern Hinduism except that, as he is associated with Vedic studies, the question could be asked of him: What inspired guidance in Vedic studies may one expect in the absence of the *ṛṣiṣ*. Perhaps the answer offered would be identical with the one found in a 'striking passage' in the *Nirukta* (XIII.12.13):

> When the ṛṣis were flying up, human beings asked gods, 'who among us will now become a *ṛṣi?*' The gods gifted this *tarka-ṛṣi* to men. The *tarka* so given was that which was drawn out by inference from reflection on the meaning of the mantras. Therefore, whatever a learned man infers (arrives through abhyūha) becomes sageness (*ārṣam*).[22]

There is one development in modern Hinduism, however, which does relate to Brahmā, albeit indirectly. It is represented by the rise of the Brahma Kumārī movement. Although this movement does not consider itself as falling within the ambit of Hinduism, anthropologists have taken note of the fact that everyone else seems to consider it a Hindu movement.[23]

[22] Murty, K. Satchidananda, *Vedic Hermeneutics*, Delhi: Motilal Banarsidass, 1993, p. 29; also see *The Cultural Heritage of India*, Vol. I, Calcutta: The Ramakrishna Mission Institute of Culture, 1958, p. 323.

[23] Babb, Lawrence A., *Redemptive Encounters: Three Modern Styles in the Hindu Tradition*, Berkeley: University of California Press, 1986, p. 5.

One may therefore proceed with this caveat in mind. It traces its origins to Dada Lekhraj (1876–1969) who was a lifelong vegetarian and teetotaler. Around the age of sixty, however, he had a series of revelations in which the imminent destruction of the world was an important theme. He felt that 'he was being given *gītā gyān*, the true "knowledge" of the Bhagavad Gītā.'[24] Under his influence, others also started entering states of *dhyāna*, and they constituted the nucleus around which a group was formed in 1937 at Hyderabad in Sind. The movement relocated in Karachi to avoid local hostility, where Lekhraj also revealed that 'he himself was Brahmā (the creator-deity of the Hindu pantheon) and the agency of the lord's creation of the new world.'[25] After Partition, the movement shifted its centre to Mount Abu in 1950, which remains its centre.

In this movement, known as the Brahma Kumārī movement, we have the rare instance of a new movement being associated with the god Brahmā, whose worship has virtually disappeared from Hinduism. Yet, in this movement, 'Lekhraj is identified with this deity and is regarded as the "father" of the movement members. Kumārī can also be rendered as "maiden" or "princess".... These meanings are consistent with the movement's teachings. A female member of the sect is a *Brahmā Kumārī*; a male member *Brahmā Kumār*.'[26] It claims a membership of about 100,000[27], and has branches in Europe, the United States and Australia, with about 800 centres[28] in all.

The association of Brahmā with this movement is a matter of some interest because Brahmā has a strong connection with Vedic studies in the Hindu imagination. The movement, however, places no special emphasis on the Vedas. The emphasis rests, rather, on meditation—hence this expectation is belied. Brahmā is also closely associated with celibacy in Hinduism, and this expectation is dramatically fulfilled

[24] *Ibid.*, p. 100.
[25] *Ibid.*, p. 103.
[26] *Ibid.*, p. 94 note 1.
[27] *Ibid.*, p. 94.
[28] *Ibid.*, p. 95.

because 'absolute celibacy... is the *sine qua non* of the virtuous life as understood by the Brahma Kumārīs,'[29] which may also explain the singlemindedness with which they seek converts.[30]

Another connection with Brahmā is provided by the millenarian nature of the movement. Millenarian movements are not unknown in Hinduism, with the Kalkī avatāra itself representing one form of it although, typically, Hindu movements do not tend to be apocalyptic in the way they tend to be in the Abrahamic religions. However, as the 'imminence of universal doom',[31] is a key element in the teaching, it is easy to see why Brahmā, as the creator of a new world after its end, would play an important role in the movement.

Brahmā became the object of censure, especially by missionaries, on account of the stories of the incestuous relation with his daughter Sarasvatī. 'The essential story is that the god Brahmā feels passion for his daughter and attempts to sleep with her. As a consequence, Śiva, in the form of the terrible Bhairava, cuts off Brahmā's fifth head [which had sprouted to ogle at her] with his thumb-nail. The head does not leave Bhairava's hand, so he wanders around various pilgrimage sites (*tīrtha*) until he reaches Varanasi where the skull falls at the Kapālamocana ('freed from the skull') tīrṭha; Śiva is then freed from the sin of brahmanicide.'[32] However, Brahmā is punished in the story itself and, according to one view, his worship was discontinued on account of the incident, so the mud does not quite stick.

[29] *Ibid.*, p. 119.

[30] *Ibid.*, pp. 94, 105.

[31] *Ibid.*, p. 109.

[32] Flood, Gavin, *An Introduction to Hinduism*, Cambridge: Cambridge University Press, 1996, p. 157.

VIII

Viṣṇu

Modern Hinduism seeks to relate science and religion with an eagerness not found in many other traditions. Whatever be the reasons underlying this phenomenon, it may itself be the reason why the doctrine of evolution has been juxtaposed with that of the incarnations of Viṣṇu by some Hindu thinkers. The procedure is not as arbitrary as might appear, if one recognizes an evolutionary pattern in the series of the Ten Incarnations to begin with—an aquatic emergence of life represented by fish (*matsya*); the amphibian by a tortoise (*kūrma*); move to land by the boar (*varāha*); the transition from animal to human form in the man-lion (*nara-siṁḥa*); the human species as pygmies in the dwarf (*vāmana*); the violent etiology of culture in Rāma with the axe (Paraśurāma); and with the introduction of chivalry in Rāma with the bow (Rāmacandra). The transition then continues from nature to culture in Kṛṣṇa, with its humanization by Buddha, and the denouement with Kalkī.

This involves a blending of two mythogems: the descent *and* ascent of Viṣṇu. Thus, Viṣṇu *descends* into the world as an incarnation but, at the same time, his incarnations *ascend* on a evolutionary gradient when the series is considered as a whole.

The two most popular incarnations of Viṣṇu continue to be Rāma and Kṛṣṇa in modern Hinduism. But they are in some ways perceived rather differently in modern Hinduism in comparison with the past. The most favoured vehicle of Rāma's popularity in the north continues to be the recitation of the Rāmakathā, specially in the form of Tulsīdās's Rāmāyaṇa. However, the introduction of TV has added a whole new dimension to the accessibility of the masses to the epic. The Rāmāyaṇa was broadcast on national television in seventy-eight episodes in 1987 and 1988. Christophe Jaffrelot writes:

> The dramatic popularity of the serials among viewers indicated how highly esteemed was Ram, especially in North India. In certain cases, watching the weekly episodes was considered as an act of devotion. Some Hindus, responding to the image of Ram on screen as if they were receiving *darshan* from god, greeted him by performing *pujas* before the television set. Following the *Ramayana*, the *Mahabharata* was shown in 91 episodes; its success led in turn to all activity being suspended on Sunday mornings when the broadcast was taking place—the average audience was estimated at 91% of those owning TV sets.[33]

Just as the popular depiction of Rāma has taken on a new dimension through the televised Rāmāyaṇa, a new perception of Kṛṣṇa has also been reinforced with the televisation of the Mahābhārata. The Kṛṣṇa of the medieval times is a romantic rather than a heroic figure, and associated more in the popular mind with Rādhā than the Gītā. But, beginning with his fresh presentation as a modern heroic type by Bankim Chandra Chatterjee, Kṛṣṇa in the modern mind is now associated with the Mahābhārata and the stirring call to action he delivers to a despondent Arjuna on the battlefield of Kurukṣetra.[34]

Vaiṣṇavism, in general, thus continues to be a major component of modern Hinduism.

> Vaiṣṇavism has not lost its attraction in our time. Not only do the centuries-old *sampradāyas* continue and intensify their activities, new movements have also arisen to reactivate *saṁkīrtan* and regular *pūjā.*

[33] Jaffrelot, Christophe, *The Hindu Nationlist Movement in India*, New York: Columbia University Press, 1996, p. 389.

[34] Sharpe, Eric J., 'The Study of Hinduism—The Setting', in *The Study of Hinduism*, Arvind Sharma (ed.), Columbia, South Carolina: University of South Carolina Press, 2003, pp. 34–5.

Swami Rāma Tīrtha has carried the message of Lord Viṣṇu to the West, and Swāmi Viṣṇupāda Bhakti Vedānta founded in ISKCON, a mission to propagate Gauḍīya-Vaiṣṇavism, not only in India but throughout the whole world. An Englishman, who under his Indian name Kṛṣṇa Prem became the guru of Indian as well as Western *bhaktas*, may still be rather exceptional, but there is no denying the fact that Vaiṣṇavism, in its many forms, with its basic message of love, has universal appeal to religiously minded persons. In late 1992 the first issue of a quarterly *Journal of Vaiṣṇava Studies* under the general editorship of S.J. Rosen began to appear from Brooklyn, New York. Its booklength issues carry important scholarly as well as devotional articles and the new journal is likely to stimulate research and disseminate knowledge on this major religion associated with the name of Viṣṇu.[35]

One should note that among all the incarnations of Viṣṇu, Kṛṣṇa had rather bad press in the early nineteenth century, and was roundly criticized by Raja Ram Mohun Roy—to say nothing of the missionaries—for his licentiousness. It was largely due to the efforts of Bankim Chandra Chatterjee (1838–94) that the Kṛṣṇa in modern Hinduism possesses a profile very different from the Kṛṣṇa in medieval Hinduism. In his *Krishnacarita* (1886, 2nd ed. 1892), he depicted Kṛṣṇa as the 'ideal man'.[36] Other writers, such as Nobin Chandra Sen and S.C. Mukhopadhyaya, continued the tradition. 'Throughout this literature, Krishna was presented along the lines laid down by Bankim Chandra as a hero, a philosopher-statesman, an example for emulation and above all as a spiritual champion of the people of India in her time of trial.'[37]

[35] Klostermaier, Klaus K., *op. cit.*, p. 260.

[36] Sharpe, Eric J., *The Universal Gītā: Western Images of the Bhagavadgītā*, London: Duckworth, 1985, p. 75.

[37] *Ibid.*

IX

Śiva

Śiva was a popular god in classical Hinduism and continues to be so in modern Hinduism—but for perhaps slightly different reasons. In fact, modern Hinduism even seems to review the reasons assigned for his popularity in its classical phase. The popular view is that the name Śiva is 'only euphemistic' and was used in an apotropaic manner.[38] However, it has been suggested on the basis of Nīlakaṇṭhas's commentary on the Mahābhārata XII.284 that the change of name from Rudra to Śiva may be explained differently: 'A truly divine power cannot in itself be malignant; and whatever dread it may inspire'—like a school teacher—'should be ascribed to a sense of sin in man. It is the recognition of this truth', according to M. Hiriyanna, 'that in all probability explains the change in the title of the deity'.[39]

More significant from the point of view of modern Hinduism are a few other considerations. Klaus K. Klostermaier points out that:

While the popularity of Śaivism in India was never seriously in doubt since it found acceptance by Vedic orthodoxy and while Śaivism pro-

[38] Klostermaier, Klaus K., *A Survey of Hinduism* (second edition), Albany, N.Y.: State University of New York Press, 1994, p. 263; M. Hiriyanna, *Outlines of Hinduism*, London: George Allen & Unwin, 1932, p. 97, note 2.

[39] *Ibid.*, p. 97.

vided the background to much of India's speculative theology, from the *Śvetāśvatara Upaniṣad* to Kāśmīr Śaivism, from Śaṅkara to Śaiva Siddhānta, the intense interest for Śaivism among western scholars is something new. Śaivism used to be the form of Hinduism upon which most abuse was heaped by early Western observers: imagine the worship of the phallus, the ritual slaughtering of animals, the frenzied dancing![40]

Klostermaier's plausible conjecture is that:

All this new sympathy for Śiva may have to do with the more liberal attitude toward sexuality that developed in the West in the past twenty years as well as the experience of terror and the dark attraction to horror so evident in contemporary films and TV plays. It is only to be hoped that besides Śiva the Terrible also Śiva the Graceful exert his influence.[41]

It is also possible to associate the popularity of Śiva to a new development in modern Hinduism that led to the abolition of the *devadāsī* system. In the process of its abolition, however, the art forms that had been nurtured by the devadāsīs were rescued from oblivion by pioneers such as Rukmani Arundale. This revival of a modern version of dance also contributed to the popularity of Śiva as not only the patron and pattern of *yogīs*, but also the lord of the cosmic dance, as he is so effectively portrayed in Cōḻa art. The revival of Bharata Nāṭyam, and its incorporation in dance performances, has extended the aesthetic dimension in secular circles. The philosophical richness of the symbolism of the 'dance of Shiva' might convey some flavour of the nature of this appeal. First of all, Śiva is depicted as dancing, that is in motion, like the universe that is constantly undergoing the processes of creation, maintenance, and destruction. The orb surrounding the image is supposed to convey this sense of cosmic motion. The drum in one hand denotes creation, for sound is the property of space with the appearance of which one round of creation commences. The other hands contains a tongue of flame, which represents the fiery consummation of the cosmos at the end

[40] Klostermaier, Klaus K., *A Survey of Hinduism*, p. 275.
[41] *Ibid.*

of the aeon. These two hands stretch out from the body of Śiva at the back while, out of the two hands in front, one is raised in the gesture of protection and denotes the maintenance of the cosmos. Thus, the three cosmic functions of creation, maintenance, and destruction are choreographed. His two other functions are those of concealment and liberation. The concealment is represented by the demon of forgetfulness on which one foot is firmly planted, while the second of his two hands in front points gently to his other foot which ensures the salvation of those who seek refuge there. The arm that points to it, shaped like a trunk, is reminiscent of Gaṇeśa—some even look upon the whole image of the dance of Natarāja as a visual representation of the Om sound itself.[42]

In contrast to the evocative quality of his role as Naṭarāja, the conical stone through which Śiva is represented acquired an embarrassing element when it came to be described as a phallic symbol—by the West. Mahatma Gandhi notes, perhaps significantly: 'It was in a missionary book that I first learnt that *shivalingam* had any obscene significance at all, and even now when I see a *shivalingam* neither the shape nor the association in which I see it, suggests any obscenity.'[43] But as surely as many a Hindu sees no phallic significance in the symbol, for the Western observer its phallic significance is equally unmistakable. David Smith writes as recently as in 2003: 'The linga is worshipped as the central pillar of the universe, *but it is definitely a phallus*.'[44] Klaus K. Klostermaier adopts a middle path when he writes: 'Its phallic origin is established beyond doubt, but it can also be safely said that it does not evoke any phallic associations in the minds of the worshippers.'[45]

[42] Zimmer, Heinrich, *Myths and Symbols in Indian Art and Civilization*, Joseph Campbell (ed.), New York and Evanston: Harper & Row, 1962, pp. 151–5.

[43] M.K. Gandhi, *Hindu Dharma*, Ahmedabad: Navajivan Publishing House, 1958, p. 25.

[44] Smith, David, *Hinduism and Modernity*, Malden, MA: Blackwell Publishing House, 2003, p. 119.

[45] Klostermaier, Klaus K., *op. cit.*, p. 143.

There is some evidence to suggest a phallic association, but a considerable body of evidence points in a different direction to which modern Hindu scholars have drawn attention. Nilakanta Sastri writes for instance:

IS ŚIVALIṄGA A PHALLIC SYMBOL?

Is the *śivaliṅga* a phallus? The discovery of phallic cult objects here and there, bearing evidence of the worship of the phallus among pre-historic tribes, has led to the easy assumption that the *śivaliṅga* was phallic in its origin. And the preponderance, real or supposed, of orgiastic rites in some form of Śāktism has doubtless sometimes influenced modern students of Śaivism into accepting an exclusively phallic interpretation of the *śivaliṅga*. But the *liṅga* may have been in origin no more than just a symbol of Śiva, as the *śālagrāma* is of Viṣṇu. The worship of the *liṅga* as a symbol once started, there was little to prevent a confusion in the popular mind between this and the cult of the phallus, and legends came to be invented of the origin of the worship of the *liṅga* as the phallus of Śiva. In some such way we can explain the passages—not many after all, and rather late in the *Mahābhārata* and other works—which lend colour to the phallic interpretation of the *śivaliṅga*. 'Of all the representations of the deity which India has imagined,' observes Barth, 'these (*liṅgas*) are perhaps the least offensive to look at. Anyhow, they are the least materialistic; and if the common people make fetishes of them, it is nevertheless true that the choice of these symbols by themselves to the exclusion of every other image was, on the part of certain founders of sects, such as Basava, a sort of protest against idolatry.' The Pallava Mahendravarman, who set up a *liṅga* in Tiruchirappalli (Trichinopoly), centuries before Basava's time, gave unmistakable expression to the very same idea.[46]

A Hindu scholar of the stature of Tartateertha Laxmanshastri Joshi has proposed a very different origin of the śivaliṅga as follows:

The origin of Rudrābhiśeka meaning sprinkling of water on the image of Rudra-Śiva, can likewise be traced back to the ritual of agnicayana. The ritual named vasordhāra has been included in agnicayana. Melted

[46] Nilakanta Sastri, K.A., 'A Historical Sketch of Śavism', in *The Cultural Heritage of India*, Haridas Bhattacharyya (ed.), Vol. IV, Calcutta: The Ramakrishna Mission Institute of Culture, 1956, pp. 67–8.

butter is poured on the altar with mantras in praise of Rudra. Most of the important symbols and rituals in the ancient Śaivadharma can thus be found in the ritual of agnicayana. Even the notion of Śaivadharma would seem to have a close resemblance to a few specified shapes of the altars for the agnicayana. The altar named nāciketacayana resembles the shape of a large Śivaliṅga. Some more shapes prescribed for construction of altars for the agnicayana, for example the cakraciti (a round solid cylinder) are remindful of the Śivaliṅga.[47]

The śivaliṅga could become the lightning rod in the recent controversy about the role of psychoanalysis in the study of Hinduism—should the psychoanalytical approach to the study of religion stake the claim that it is phallic in essence. This controversy around the use of psychoanalysis in Hinduism has now become so fierce that a leading Western scholar who advocates it even had to cancel a scheduled lecture in Bombay.[48]

[47] Joshi, Tarkateertha Laxmanshastri, *Development of Indian Culture: Vedas to Gandhi*, S.R. Nene (tr), Mumbai: Lok Vangmaya Griha, 2001, p. 293.

[48] Braveman, Amy M., 'The Interpretations of Gods: Do Leading Religious Scholars Err in Their Analysis of Hindu Texts', *University of Chicago Magazine*, 97:2:33 (December 2004).

X

Jīva

It is not easy to be born as a human being in the course of one's existence as a jīva. Indeed, 'some expositors of Hinduism have worked out fantastically lengthy programs of incarnations, e.g., according to some a jīva is granted a human body only after going through 8,400,000 previous incarnations—2,000,000 as a plant, 900,000 as an aquatic creature, 1,100,000 as an insect, 1,000,000 as a bird, 3,000,000 as a cow, and 400,000 as a monkey.'[49] Such is the picture in classical Hinduism. Modern Hinduism is much more optimistic in this respect, maximally expressed in the Theosophical belief that one does not slide back from human birth.

It is the jīva that transmigrates in saṁsāra in accordance with karma. This is the classical view, and persists in modern Hinduism. However, a fresh understanding of the doctrines of karma and saṁsāra in modern Hinduism create room for a new look at the jīva. The classical vision itself supplies the starting point. The usual analysis of karma bifurcates its working in terms of *phala* and *saṁskāra*:[50] the actual result the action produces, and the psychic residue it leaves behind. It

[49] Wilson Organ, Troy, *The Hindu Quest for the Perfection of Man*, p. 121, note 27.

[50] Hiriyanna, M., *The Essentials of Indian Philosophy*, pp. 47–9.

is these residues that fuel the process of continuous rebirth, and hence hold the key to the process. In other words, it is saṁskāra that holds the key to saṁsāra.

The jīva possesses three bodies, according to classical Hinduism: (1) the gross body; (2) the subtle body, and (3) the causal body. As far as the working out of the karmic results are concerned, the subtle body is the most significant; it is the one that leaves one body and enters another, and corresponds to the *liṅga śarīra* of the Sāṅkhya school. This has virtually led to the neglect of the causal body, with the psychological dimension of life receiving increasing attention in modern Hinduism. It is quite likely, however, that the causal body will never entirely drop out of sight, as it is 'the causal body which contains within itself all the characteristics and tendencies (samskāra) of the creature in the seed-state as it were, as the seed is causally related to the tree, so is this body to the life and career of a creature. That is why it is said to be the causal body.'[51]

It might be an insight of modern Hinduism to connect phala with the subtle body and saṁskāra with the causal body when it comes to the operation of karma.

[51] Swami Nirvedananda, *Hinduism at a Glance*, Calcutta: Ramakrishna Mission Calcutta Student's Home, 1969, p. 184.

XI

Saṁsāra

The concept of saṁsāra in classical Hinduism was cosmological. One lived in a universe that was without beginning or end, and one assumed innumerable forms of life until one attained mokṣa. The concept of saṁsāra in classical Hinduism involved vast temporal dimensions, a sense of which is graphically conveyed by Joseph Campbell as follows:

In India, for example, where the first form to appear in the lotus of Vishṇu's dream is seen as Brahmā, it is held that when the cosmic dream dissolves, after 100 Brahmā years, its Brahmā too will disappear—to reappear, however, when the lotus again unfolds. Now one Brahmā year is reckoned as 360 Brahmā days and nights, each night and each day consisting of 12,000,000 divine years. But each divine year, in turn, consists of 360 human years; so that one full day and night of Brahmā, or 24,000,000 divine years, contains 24,000,000 times 360 or 8,640,000,000 human years, just as in our own system of reckoning the 24 hours of a day contain 86,400 seconds—each second corresponding to the length of time, furthermore, of one heartbeat of a human body in perfect physical condition. Thus it appears not only that the temporal order written on the faces of our clocks is the same as that of the Indian god Vishṇu's dream, but also that there is built into this system the mythological concept of a correspondence between the organic rhythms of the human body as a microcosm and the cycling eons of the universe, the macrocosm.[52]

[52] Campbell, Joseph, *The Mythic Image*, Princeton, N.J.: Princeton University Press, 1974, p. 141, diacritics supplied.

The approach to saṁsāra in modern Hinduism has become much more psychological, for the basis of this involvement in the temporal process are psychic dispositions. Hence the aphorism: saṁskāra *is* saṁsāra.

Modern Hinduism not only tends to psychologize the process, but also to subtilize it, for fundamentally the flow of saṁsāra from one life to another is not different from the way one day flows into another, or even the way one moment flows into another. Saṁsāra is basically to be identified with this flux.

This shift from the classical versions of the concept to the modern has not gone unnoticed by scholars. One finds the following, fully contextualized, and comprehensive presentation of it in the words of Hendrik Kraemer:

> An interesting example is to be found in the *History of Philosophy Eastern and Western*, a work in two volumes sponsored by the Ministry of Education of the Government of India on the initiative of the late Indian Minister of Education, Maulana Abul Kalam Azad. This book is an able performance, written mainly by Indian scholars of philosophy out of a sincere concern for the universal character of philosophy and the plasticity of Hindu spirituality. In the sections where Islam as represented in India comes in for consideration, the authors offer, as the right interpretation of Islam, that it advocates the fundamental unity of all faiths and the true reconciliation of religion, science and rationalism. The Indian portions are characterized by a new stress on the reality of the world, which implies a realistic interpretation of Maya and a positive attitude towards history. Also by a distinct 'recession' (to use again, as in the case of mutation, a term from modern biology) of the Indian concepts of *Karma* and *samsara*, which for centuries have been basic to Indian religious-philosophical thinking and are now reduced to general concepts in line with modern ideas (*samsara* for instance=dynamic change or flux).[53]

[53] Hendrik, Kraemer, *World Cultures and World Religions: The Coming Dialogue*, London: Lutterworth Press, 1960, pp. 360–1.

XII

Karma

I

Subtle but significant conceptual shifts have occurred in the understanding of karma in modern Hinduism. It might be helpful to number them so as not to lose track of them.

1. Karma in pre-modern Hinduism was sometimes equated with fatalism. This misconception has been effectively removed by modern Hinduism. S. Radhakrishnan regretted in 1926 that 'unfortunately the theory of karma became confused with fatality in India when man himself grew feeble and was disinclined to do his best.'[54] He tries to redress the situation by pointing out that 'The spiritual element in man allows him freedom within the limits of his nature. Man is not a mere mechanism of instincts. The spirit in him can triumph over the automatic forces that try to enslave him. The *Bhagavadgītā* asks us to raise the self by the self. We can use the material with which we are endowed to promote our ideas. The cards in the game of life are given to us. We do not select them. They are traced to our past Karma, but we can call as we please, lead what suit we will, and as we play, we gain or lose. And there is freedom.'[55]

[54] Radhakrishnan, S., *The Hindu View of Life*, p. 76.
[55] *Ibid.*, p. 75.

As in other cases, this has meant that those elements in classical Hinduism which emphasized the effectiveness of effort are highlighted in modern Hinduism, even in textbooks.[56] So far as the charge of fatalism is concerned, some modern Hindus make it stand on its head: 'The doctrine of karma teaches that man himself is the architect of his life. What he did in the past life is entirely responsible for what he is in the present life. *This is the very opposite of fatalism.* It eliminates chance or caprice....'[57]

Nevertheless it seems on the basis of some surveys that belief in fate is still widespread among modern Hindus. Philip Ashby writes:

> While it had not occurred to me, faculty and student advisers suggested that while being questioned concerning karma, students should also be asked whether they believed in fate. Seventy-one percent answered in the affirmative, 11 percent more than had said they believed in astrology and palmistry and 15 percent more than had believed in karma that passes from one life to another. It was interesting to note the number of students who ascribed to fate their success or failure in examinations, in obtaining the proper wives or husbands, and in securing various material goods. Not only were failures despite hard work laid at the door of fate, but successes without endeavor were also thought to be the result of fate.[58]

2. This emphasis on effort has led to a more dynamic conception of karma that has in turn led to the view that the results of actions, which in classical Hinduism were by and large supposed to produce their effort in another life, might well do so in this one! As Philip Ashby writes:

> In a further attempt to discover the role of central themes from the great tradition, the students were questioned about saṁsāra and karma.

[56] Chatterjee, Satischandra and Dhirendramohan Datta, *An Introduction to Indian Philosophy*, Calcutta: Calcutta University Press, 1968, p. 18, note 1.

[57] Dandekar, R.N., 'The Role of Man in Hinduism', in *The Religion of the Hindus*, Kenneth W. Morgan (ed.), New York: The Ronald Press Company, 1965, pp. 128–9.

[58] Ashby, Philip, *Modern Trends in Hinduism*, New York and London: Columbia University Press, 1974, pp. 64–5.

Fifty-seven percent of all the students believed in saṁsāra, the cycle of transmigration of the soul, with over two-thirds of those in the twice-born group doing so. Only the untouchables, with 6 out of the 10 answering negatively, had a majority who did not believe in this basic Hindu presupposition. In regard to karma, a basic distinction must be made between karma that is passed from one existence over to a later existence and karma that is passed from one moment of this life to another later time in this same life. The students wanted to make this distinction clear, with 56 percent believing in both types of karma, while a large number of those who did not believe in karma as something carrying over from one life to the next did hold that it is an active force in the successive stages of this present life.[59]

3. In the past it was sometimes thought that as a person's suffering is the outcome of his or her own karma, one is under no obligation to help the other person. It could even be construed as mischievous or sentimental tinkering with the cosmic working of the law of karma. This view has few takers now. Such a situation, in karmic terms, is increasingly viewed as an opportunity for performing good karma or practising karmayoga (or the detached performance of one's duties to others). This line of argument can also be extended to embrace a broader social context. T.M.P. Mahadevan remarks:

> Under the rigid law of *karma*, it is said, there is no room for social service; for it does not allow of interference with the working out of a man's *karma*. This is a gross misreading of the law. It goes against the grain of Hinduism to suggest that each individual is an independent entity. The individual is not unrelated to society. He acts on and is acted upon by these that surround him. And naturally he has to share their joys and sorrows. If he brings succour to the suffering it is in part to his own advantage. Social service is not only consistent with the law of *karma* but is also enjoined as a means to release from *saṁsāra*. Work, when selfish, forges the chains of bondage, and when selfless, makes for freedom from fetters; just as a poison which ordinarily kills becomes a means of cure when it has been medically purified.[60]

4. Karma has often been confused with resignation, and modern Hinduism is quite conscious of this. A certain incident

[59] *Ibid.*, p. 64.
[60] Mahadevan, T.M.P., *Outlines of Hinduism*, p. 61.

in the life of Swami Vivekananda reported by Sister Nivedita captures the point well: 'When we were at Almora, I remember a certain elderly man with a face full of amiable weakness, who came to put to him a question about Karma. What were they to do, he asked, whose Karma it was, to see the strong oppress the weak? The Swami turned on him in surprised indignation. "Why, thrash the strong, of course!" he said. "You forget your own part in this karma. Yours is always the right to rebel!"'[61]

5. The concept of collective karma has gained credibility in modern Hinduism as a result of the Hindus undergoing certain experiences as a group—such as foreign domination—that could be viewed as collective punishment for the collective sin of having participated in an inegalitarian social system for centuries. S. Radhakrishnan even advanced the hope that 'an individual will identify his own karma with the karma of all mankind.'[62] This has eschatological implications, for then it could be argued that 'an individual is not saved or liberated until he overcomes the distinction between his own salvation and the salvation of the rest of mankind.'[63] It also has universalistic implications:

> First, Radhakrishnan's interpretation emphasizes a collective unity of an individual's *karma* with the historical *karma*,. Second, he insists that the view of personal salvation needs to be transcended for the sake of universal salvation; consequently, in modern Hinduism the doctrine of karma could be interpreted in such a way that the theory of *karma* makes demands on an individual to be responsible for his own destiny and ultimately for the destiny of all mankind.[64]

6. A new idea which modern Hinduism has to integrate in its paradigm is that of evolution. Robert A. McDermott has made the fruitful suggestion that Radhakrishnan 'formulates a theory of salvation in which *karma dictates the terms of individual salvation and evolution sets the term for universal*

[61] *The Complete Works of Sister Nivedita*, Vol. I , p. 88.

[62] Harris, Ishwar C., *Radhakrishnan: Profile of a Universalist*, Calcutta: Minerva Associates [Publications] Pvt. Ltd., 1982, p. 121.

[63] *Ibid.*

[64] *Ibid.*, p. 122.

salvation.'[65] This enables one to set the law of evolution alongside the law of karma. Some modern Hindu thinkers have even suggested that 'the Hindu seers had a clear idea of what we call evolution. Patanjali, the author of the *Yoga Sūtras*, referred to it as "*jātyantara-pariṇāma*", that is, transformation of one genus or species into another. They had a definite idea about its cause, for which modern science may be said to be still groping. They held that one genus or species has within it, potentially, whatever evolves out of it.'[66]

II

It was noted earlier that modern Hinduism has had to deal with the charge that it is fatalistic. That such a charge should be brought against Hinduism in relation to the doctrine of karma is ironical, for fatalism means that what happens to us is predetermined by the goddesses called the Fates in the Graeco-Roman tradition. That is to say, someone *other* than us decides for us what is going to befall us. Even if the doctrine of karma is confused with a doctrine of predetermination, the description of it as fatalistic misses an important point. Even if what is going to happen to us is allegedly totally predetermined according to our karma, it would be erroneous in the extreme to call this condition fatalistic. The doctrine of karma holds that we undergo the consequences of our *own* actions, even if they are thoroughly predetermined. So even when we are thoroughly in the grip of predestination, it is our *own* actions in the past that are responsible, and not any agency other than us such as the Fates or even gods.

To move now from a verbal to a more substantial critique of the view that karma implies predetermination: It is true that, while according to the doctrine of karma, our experiences in life involve predetermination, the key element to determine is the *extent* of such predetermination.

[65] *Ibid.*, p. 121.

[66] Swami Nirvedananda, *Hinduism at a Glance*, p. 167.

Three broad positions can be identified on this point from within the Hindu tradition; they would be labelled as maximalist, moderate, and minimalist.

According to the maximalist position, all the external events of our life are predetermined, down to the smallest detail. This comes closest to justifying the charge that karma equals 'fatalism'. After all, karma means both action and the result of action. So, the charge then is that the actions of one's life are so thoroughly determined in advance that no room is left for the exercise of free will now, even if in some remote past our actions, whose consequences have created this state of affairs, were freely willed.

One needs to remember at this point that the word karma not only includes both—the meaning of action as well as the result of action—but also both action *as well as* reaction. According to even this maximalist version, even if all that is to take place in our life is predetermined, the *reaction* to them is not so determined; that we will experience adversity, and the exact form in which we will experience it may be predetermined, but whether we react to it with panic or fortitude is *not* predetermined. Such reaction to action is also action; in fact, it is through this action in the form of reaction that we generate the karma for our future life in this life, although what is to befall us in this life may be fully predetermined.

This is as true of actions that we are destined to *perform* in our life, under this maximalist interpretation, as of the events that are destined to *befall* us in this life. Suppose, then, that we are destined to hand over one dollar to a beggar: This is predestined. However, whether we hand over this dollar to the beggar compassionately or contemptuously is still open to us.

It is clear, therefore, that scope for the operation of free will is provided for even under the maximalist interpretation.

The moderate version of the doctrine seems to accord better with the evidence of daily life. Our existential situation is characterized by both givenness and openness. Our gender, nationality, physical features, etc., have been predetermined, as it were. However, we could learn a new language or acquire a new skill on our own volition whenever we chose to. Thus, while some dimensions of our life are characterized by givenness, others are characterized by openness. Such a realization amounts to realism rather than fatalism.

It is clear, however, that in the context of this moderate version, karma cannot be glibly equated with fatalism. The illustration of a game of cards is a happy one in this context. The hand of cards may have been dealt to us by chance, God, or previous karma. But how we play that hand still remains in our hands.

The minimalist version makes it even harder to associate karma with fatalism. According to the understanding promoted by this version, there is *really* no such thing as predetermination. If the so-called predetermination is tracked down to its source, it turns out to be a case of free-will! It is only our own freely-willed actions that, in the course of time, harden into destiny. Thus, far from being synonymous with fatalism, karma turns out to be synonymous with free will.

Those who identify karma with fatalism also betray a rather simplistic understanding of karma in Hindu thought. According to a standard trichotomy, karma is said to be of three types in Hinduism: (1) *āgāmi* or kriyamāṇa; (2) sañcita; and (3) prārabdha. To the first category of karma—āgāmi or kriyamāṇa—belong actions that we are performing now and will perform in the future. To the second category belong those karmas that are still undergoing maturation. This category consists of the inventory of our accumulated karma. To the third category belong those karmas that have already begun to produce their effect.

A homespun example could help illustrate the point. Suppose I am confronted with the option of whether to smoke or not. I may decide to start smoking or I may not. This is new or present karma. Now suppose I do decide to start smoking and go on for fifteen years. This is the stage when I am accumulating karma. Now, when I get lung cancer as a result of having smoked for fifteen years, it has become destiny. Even if I now stopped smoking, it will make no difference.

A more traditional example is provided by an archer with his quiver of arrows. The arrow that has been discharged by the archer—and which is speeding its way towards the target—is prārabdha, or destiny. The arrow that the archer holds in his hand is āgāmi or kriyamāṇa karma. He or she is free to decide whether to discharge the arrow or not, or to select the direction in which it should be discharged should one decide to do so. The bows in the quiver constitute sañcita karma.

One could then propose that our life is a combination of all these three types of karma. The error committed by those who confuse it with fatalism consists of identifying the whole concept of karma with only one category of it, namely prārabdha. It is true that one line of presentation in the tradition identifies prārabdha with that part of sañcita karma which has now begun to take effect, and thus accounts for the experiences of the present life. This would coincide with the maximalist view mentioned earlier. It is worth noting, however, that this position has typically been developed in response to *another* problem—namely, that if realization results in annihilation of all karma, on the one hand, and the realized person (who by definition is free from karma) continues to exist after realization, on the other, then how is his or her continued existence to be accounted for? The answer is given as follows: when such a person attains realization, all the accumulated karma is destroyed, while no new karma is generated as the realized person possesses no ego to which it could attach itself. His or her continued existence is then explained as a result of the working out of prārabdha—or that karma which gave rise to this existence. Just as a potter's wheel continues to spin for a while even after one has stopped imparting any motion to it, so does the realized person's life wind down. If he or she is seen to be doing something, or something is seen happening to him, it is the consequence of this residual karma of prārabdha—comparable to the inertial motion of the wheel.

The point to note is that the triple distinction of karma is applied in this way to address the question of the continued existence of the *realized one* rather than to address the question of fate and free will in the case of ordinary human beings, although it could conceivably be applied to their case also.

If this were the case, the freedom to react would still be available.

In other words, no matter how we try to skin the cat of karma, it still comes out alive, with free will. This should not be surprising if we take one fundamental factor into account in the light of Hinduism: Human beings are *conscious* human beings and consciousness is ever free, in the sense that it is possible for one to think of anything, for it to flow in any direction, or to receive any new impression. Karma cannot involve fatalism, because being human involves possessing such a consciousness, whose quicksilver quality eludes any predeterministic pinning down of it.

Two points are often lost sight of in discussions of karma, and this contributes to a fatalistic understanding of it. The first is that the doctrine pertains as much to what we *do* as to what happens to us. Most of the time it is invoked to explain what happens to us—and in this context, it is then argued that what happened was the inescapable consequence of our own past deeds. However, the doctrine also implies, by the same token, that when we set out to achieve something our success is inevitable too—if we keep at it! All obstacles will be overcome in time. Thus, if we insist on using the term fatalism when we view ourselves at the receiving end of karma, then we will have to use the term *triumphalism* when we are at the cutting edge of it.

This brings up the second point. The doctrine of karma is typically discussed in Hindu thought in the context of mokṣa, that is to say, the achievement of mokṣa. Karma then, in this context represents *sādhanā* or spiritual effort, in one sense, and the saṁsaric world in which we are involved as a result of our part karma, in the other. That is to say, the concept of karma in the context of mokṣa is as much forward-looking as backward-looking, if not more.

An illustration may clarify the point. If I fall down after stumbling, I could blame my fall on the law of gravitation. However, the astronauts also deal with the same law of gravitation—but their focus of interest lies in trying to get beyond the range of Earth's gravitational pull rather than using it to explain why we fall when we slip. The interest of the astronauts is in the *law* of gravitation as a whole, rather than in specific instances of its operation, and it is the operational field of the law they wish to transcend. Similarly, the seeker of liberation wants to transcend the operational field of karma as such, or the *law* of karma, if you will. Just as the astronaut experiences weightlessness as a result of having gone beyond the gravitational pull of the earth, the spiritual aspirant hopes to achieve 'karmalessness', as a result of having gone beyond the range of the pull of karma.

It is as fatuous to assume that one cannot do anything because one is bound by karma as it is to assume that one must remain glued to one's chair because of the law of gravitation. Both laws give general insights into the nature of our existence—they identify the overall contexts in which our actions are performed, and offer an explanation of the factors by which they are governed. They indicate the limitations our movements are subject to, and must not be misread as doctrines of immobilization.

The fact that the doctrine of karma is discussed in the context of mokṣa, which is concerned with the *spiritual* dimension of human existence, leads one to re-emphasize the fact that the 'spirit' of a human being cannot be trapped, no more than sunlight can be chained or the wind be fettered.

India has, in practice, sometimes confused bad management with destiny, but it is just that—a confusion. This confusion is not confined to India, as the following excerpt demonstrates: It deals with the dismissal of Glenn Hoddle, the coach of England's soccer team, 'a born-again Christian who has never made a secret of religious views that include a belief in reincarnation and spiritual healing.'[67]

> 'You and I have been physically given two hands and two legs and half-decent brains,' Hoddle told *The Times* of London. 'Some people have not been born like that for a reason. The karma is working from another lifetime.'

[67] Lyall, Sarah, 'Hoddle, Coach of England, Is Dismissed', in The *New York Times*, 3 February 1999, p. C29.

He added that everyone pays the price for previous lives, saying: 'What you sow, you have to reap.'

The remarks raised an immediate outcry from groups who represent disabled people and from the Government of Prime Minister Tony Blair. The government's Minister for Sports, Tony Banks, said that Hoddle's remarks had been so embarrassing that 'it would be best if Glenn just walked.'

Even Blair weighed in, saying that if Hoddle had been quoted accurately, 'it would be very difficult for him to stay' in his job.

Hoddle had met with F.A. officials to try to save his job, and his 13-year-old daughter, Zara, sent a letter to the British Broadcasting Corporation with a plea.

'I think this situation is the most pathetic reason for someone to maybe lose their job and to have so much hassle over,' she wrote. 'If you would take time to listen to what his explanation is then maybe you would understand it a bit more.'

Trying desperately to salvage the situation, Hoddle gave a series of interviews in which he said that he had long supported and worked on behalf of the disabled. And he tried further to clarify his views on past lives, saying that he 'was not some crackpot who just comes out with stupid reasons to cause controversy' and that *The Times* had unfairly quoted him out of context in a long interview that was supposed to be about sports.

'The idea that we have all lived before and that those who were wicked or evil in past lives are not blessed with happy lives when they come back is not mine,' he said. 'Believe me, reincarnation was not something invented by Glenn Hoddle. I'm not sure about it, but some of it makes more sense than just dismissing the unfairness in life as the luck of the draw.'[68]

One might ask, coming to it from a context which accuses Hinduism of being karmically fatalistic: 'What is wrong with this statement?'

One thing wrong with this statement is intuited, but not articulated, by *Time* magazine, when it announced the news as follows:

Instant Bad Karma

Having opined that the disabled are 'paying for the sins of an earlier life,' England's national soccer coach Glenn Hoddle paid for his own

[68] *Ibid.*

verbal transgressions last week—when, following a great public uproar, he was sacked by the English Football Association.[69]

In other words, it is not just a matter of the other person's karma, but also your own which becomes implicated in it as your attitude towards it. To use the doctrine of karma as a way of blaming the victim, as a form of scapegoating, generates its own brand of bad karma.

Even in terms of the general doctrine of karma rather than in the context of specific acts of karma, the statement is misleading, at least on two counts. First, in many discussions of karma, it is said to constitute an element in the outcome—only in extreme versions of it does it constitute the only element. But, and this is the second point, even if such be the case, a crucial point is being overlooked. The doctrine of karma makes two connections: it connects the past to the present and *the present to the future.* The problem with the kind of statements made by Hoddle is that it only connects the past with the present—and stops there.

A third point is also involved: There is the failure here to connect karma with dharma. The point is not so much that 'That is his karma'; the point, rather, is: 'Given that that is his karma, what is my dharma?'

[69] *Time,* 15 February 1999, p. 7.

XIII

Dharma

I

Dharma is a key concept in the Hindu worldview, one with a deep cultural resonance. Let us begin by recognizing this fact first.

Several years ago, I read an account by an Australian journalist of her trip to India. During its course, she visited Fatehpur Sikri—the city near Agra that was built by Akbar as the capital of his empire but later abandoned for reasons not entirely clear, although lack of adequate water supply has often been offered as one.

Amidst these magnificent ruins, some young men eked out a living by diving from great stoney heights into deep pools of water, for a consideration. The Australian journalist remarked how, after witnessing such a steep plunge, she offered the stipulated amount to the young man with the remark: 'But don't you think that it's a bit degrading?' he replied with exquisite dignity (her words), 'But Madam, this is my *dharma*!'

The use of this word by Ramaṇa Maharṣi, who died in 1950, gives rise to a more intriguing issue. He lived in an ashram on a sacred hill in south India, which was disturbed one night by the arrival of thieves. The thieves, disappointed by their takings from the public cash-box, began belabouring the residents under the impression that they had hidden the assets of the ashram—they did not spare even the sage, whom they hit with a wooden pole (*lathi*) on one leg. Thereupon, the sage proffered the other leg, explaining his act to his puzzled assailants: 'As you have hit me on one leg, of which there are two, you might as well hit the other one for the sake of maintaining symmetry.'

After the intruders left, his followers discussed the question of reporting the matter to the police, but Ramaṇa Maharṣi put the matter to rest, saying: 'They are thieves. It is their dharma to steal. We are renunciants. It is our dharma to forgive. Let each follow their own dharma.'

The word dharma is from the root *dhṛ*, which means 'to uphold'. Therefore, anything that upholds an individual, a society, a polity, even the cosmos, is its dharma. Dharma is what makes a thing what it is, either descriptively or prescriptively.

This idea that dharma constitutes the inherent nature of a thing is important, especially as it involves a distinction between the inherent and the adventitious properties of a thing. Take water, for example. It is the property of water to be cold. So when we take a glass of cool water, we do not ask: 'Why is it cool?' We do, however, ask: 'Why is it hot?', if we find that the water in the glass is hot. Upon inquiry, we may be able to identify an external cause that accounts for its heat. Note that such an explanation is not required when the water is cool. Moreover, efforts have to be made to keep hot water warm, otherwise it tends to cool. Note further that 'mere efflux of time is sufficient'[70] to cool it. Thus, its heat 'comes from an external cause. And, for going cool it does not need an external cause.'[71] In contrast, heat is the inherent property of fire. If the heat goes on diminishing and goes out, you say 'the fire has gone out. You don't say the heat has gone out.' But with regard to water, it was different. When the heat went out you

[70] Swami Bharati Krishna Tirtha, *Sanathan Dharma*, Bombay: Bharatiya Vidya Bhavan, 1985, p. 174.

[71] *Ibid.*

did not say the water had gone out, you said the heat had gone out'[72] because it was adventitious to it. Also note that water possesses the property of putting out fire, and even *hot* water possesses that property.

The million-dollar question is: How do we find out what is the dharma in a particular context? The discussion of dharma—in the sense of what is the right thing to do under a given set of circumstances—pervades Hindu literature.

The following four sources of dharma are listed in classical Hinduism:

(1) Śruti, or Revelation; (2) *Smṛti*, or Tradition; (3) *Ācāra*, or Exemplary Conduct; and (4) *Ātmatuṣṭi*, or Conscience.

This list can be viewed in at least three ways. According to one perspective, each of the four items could be viewed as a source of dharma (*dharmamūla*) in its own right, independently of the other.

The dominant perspective arguably in classical Hinduism was a second one, according to which the list represents a hierarchy. Thus, in the quest for what is the dharma in a particular situation, one first consulted Revelation. If no answer was forthcoming, one consulted Tradition, then Ācāra, and finally took recourse to one's own conscience.

Modern Hinduism has developed a third view of this scheme, which gives the primary role to conscience, in a sort of last-shall-be-first manner. This is best exemplified by Mahatma Gandhi, who was building on an earlier tradition of modern Hinduism, which has accepted the Vedas but rejected Vedic infallibility.[73] In general, although its literalness was upheld by such a major figure as Swami Dayānanda Sarasvatī[74], modern Hinduism has emphasized the spirit over the letter of the law.

[72] *Ibid.*

[73] See M.K. Gandhi, *Hindu Dharma*, Bharatan Kumarappa (ed.), Ahmedabad: Navajivan Press, 1958, p. 299; Arvind Sharma, *The Concept of Universal Religion in Modern Hindu Thought*, London: Macmillan, 1998, pp. 29–31.

[74] *Ibid.*

Gandhi openly declared that he would reject any scriptural command opposed to common sense and conscience, and in this one could see the influence of the moral individualism of the West. The principle, however, was not free from problems. How was one to distinguish the voice of conscience from one's whim or veiled self-interest? How did one know that one was hearing the voice of God, and not that of the Devil? After all, Keshub Chunder Sen (1838–84) had also subscribed to the doctrine of *ādeśa*, or what was revealed to one in one's heart. On the basis of this ādeśa, he had gone ahead with the marriage of his daughter against the wishes of many members of the Brāhmo Samaj, resulting in its split.[75]

Gandhi's position on the matter of conscience therefore needs to be understood carefully. It possesses two dimensions—one metaphysical, the other moral. Absolute truth was indeed absolute, but a human being could not have unqualified access to it as a human being, because of the limitations of being a human being. Thus, all one could hope to have access to was relative truth, metaphysically speaking. But the *moral* authority of such relative truth was absolute and binding on one, as perceived at the time. To the question: But how do I know it is true because it is relative? Gandhi's answer was: If it appears to one as the truth at the time, it is the right thing to do, even if *subsequently* one realizes that it was not the 'truth', or has to change one's position. The *truth* as perceived at the time, although relative, is the *right* thing to do. He was fond of quoting Confucius on this point: 'To know what is right and not to do it, is cowardice.' It does not matter if, later, one's concept of what is right changed.

There was in fact no way of knowing *at the time* whether one had the truth, for only by its 'fruits ye shall know it'. There were, however, ways of increasing the probability that what one heard was the voice of God, and not otherwise. Leading a clean moral life was one such way.

It is also here that Gandhi's teachings on truth and non-violence converge in the context of dharma. For, if one pursued

[75] *Ibid.*, pp. 33–4.

one's truth through non-violence, and it turned out that one was mistaken about the truth, then one would have only harmed oneself, and not others; if one turned out to be right, then again, it was far better that the cause be advanced through non-violence anyway. The fact that Jesus Christ both claimed to preach the truth *and* carried the Cross could be read as a metaphorical statement of this fact.

The discussion of dharma can branch out in many directions.

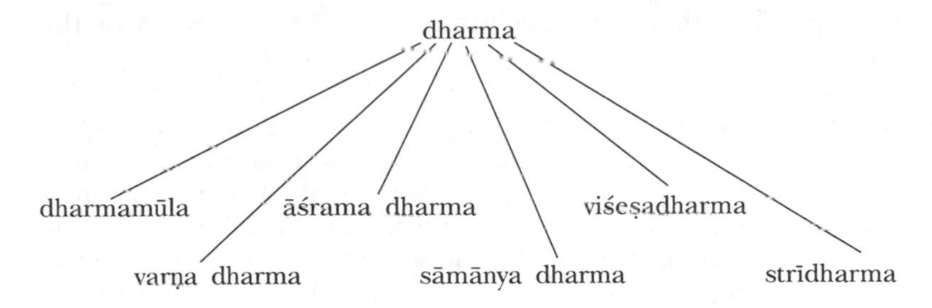

II

The word dharma also took on a fresh significance in modern Hinduism once it was juxtaposed with the English word 'religion'. This is significant because 'the use of the Islamic concept of religion, *dīn*, as an Arabic-Persian analogue of dharma, had no comparable consequences.'[76] This is already apparent in the work of Bankim Chandra Chatterjee (1838–94), and finds further extension in the work of S.V. Ketkar (1884–1937).[77] In his *Dharmatattva*,[78] Bankim Chandra Chatterjee makes a point that was destined to become part and parcel of modern Hindu thought. As far as Hindus are concerned:

For religion they had no name, because the Hindu never entertained any conception to which such a name would have been applicable. With

[76] Halbfass, Wilhelm, *India and Euorpe: An Essay in Understanding*, Albany, NY: State University of New York Press, 1988, p. 340. Punctuation supplied.

[77] *Ibid.*, p. 346.

[78] For an English translation, see Bankim Chandra Chatterjee, *The Essentials of Dharma*, Calcutta: Sribhumi Pub. Co., 1977.

other peoples, religion is only a part of life; there are things religious and there are things lay and secular. To the Hindu, his whole life was religion.[79]

From this to the Supreme Court judgement upholding Hinduism as a 'way of life' is but a step.[80]

This churning around the word dharma becomes clear when we subject a term such as *sanātana dharma* to a comprehensive exploration. One begins with the familiar point about Hindus not having a word for religion, but this time the point is applied to their *own* religion. A.L. Basham writes of the Hindus:

Though they form one of the largest and most important religious groups of the world, their faith is indefinable in a few words. It is possible to define the Christian or Muslim as the man who attempts to follow what he believes to be the teachings of Christ or Muhammad respectively, but Hinduism had no such single founder. Some modern sociologists have defined Christians and Muslims as those who consider themselves such, but a similar definition cannot be applied to Hindus, for probably most of them have never even heard the word Hindu, and have no name for their own religion.[81]

Some have gone further, and claimed that there is no such thing as Hinduism. It seems to me that these people are in denial; and A.L. Basham has simply overstated the point that Hindus are now widely known by a name they did not originally use themselves. The Hindus do have a name for their own religion—and it is sanātana dharma.

Before we begin to consider the ways in which sanātana dharma may be understood, let us be clear about the ways in which it should not be understood. These are two, to begin with:

(1) The nineteenth century witnessed the rise of a movement called the Ārya Samāj, led by Swami Dayānanda Sarasvatī

[79] Cited, Wilhelm Halbfass, *op. cit.*, p. 339.

[80] Sharma, Arvind, 'What Is Hinduism?', in *The Study of Hindusim*, Arvind Sharma (ed.), p. 12.

[81] Basham, A.L., 'Hinduism', in *The Concise Encyclopedia of Living Faiths*, R.C. Zaehner (ed.), Boston: Beacon Press, 1967, p. 225.

(1824–83). This movement opposed many traditional Hindu practices, such as image-worship, caste-discrimination, and so on. Those who opposed the reformist plank of the Ārya Samāj came to be referred to as *Sanātanī Hindus.* The controversy has virtually died down, and the social (as opposed to the theological) reformist agenda of the Ārya Samāj is now part of the national consensus. This use of the word indicates its involvement in the sectarian clashes within Hinduism—and one would be well advised to steer clear of it here.

(2) This second understanding is not unconnected with the first. Those Hindus who stood by the traditional practices thought that such hoary practices should not be changed. They supported this claim by maintaining that the word *sanātana* in the expression sanātana dharma meant 'unchanging'—therefore, as followers of sanātana dharma, they were committed to an unchanging life-style. Even those not engaged in controversies with the Ārya Samāj sometimes took the word in this sense.[82]

[82] Walker, Benjamin, *The Hindu World*, Vol. I, New York: Frederick A. Praeger, 1968, p. 445. P.V. Kane clarifies the point as follows: 'When reforms are suggested in these days, conservative people put forward the plea that ours is "sanātana-dharma" and so no changes should be introduced. But the words "sanātana dharma" do not mean that dharma always stands still or is immutable; all that those words mean is that our culture is very ancient and has a long tradition behind it but they do not mean that dharma permits no change. As a matter of fact, fundamental changes in conceptions, beliefs, and practices have been made from ancient times to the medieval times by means of various devices. Attention may be drawn to a few. Veda was all in all in very ancient times, but in the Upaniṣads this was changed, the Muṇḍaka I.1.5 designating the four Vedas as inferior knowledge (aparā vidyā) and the knowledge of the immutable *Brahman* as the higher vidyā; in the Chān. Up. VII.1.4 the four Vedas and several other branches of knowledge are called by Sanatkumāra (whom Nārada approached for instruction) merely by name (*nāma*). Yajñas were the most important religious practice in the early Vedic period, but the Muṇḍaka Up. I.2.7 designates them as leaky boats and regards those who hold them as the best thing to be fools. Vide above pp. 1265–72 about changes in the views on *anuloma* marriages, on the topic of whose food may be partaken even by a brāhmaṇa, the abrogation of many Vedic practices by the doctrine of Kalivarja (matters forbidden in Kali age) &c. Manu, Yāj.,

Despite these clarifications, the description of Hinduism as sanātana-dharma has also been, or can be, criticized for other reasons.

(1) Gavin Flood writes: 'The nineteenth-century Hindu reformers speak of Hinduism as the eternal religion (sanātana-dharma), a common idea among modern Hindus today in their self-description.'[83] The impression created is that it is a new-fangled term. Wilhelm Halbfass has gone the furthest in arguing this point:

To be sure, the expression *sanātanadharma* (*dharmaḥ sanātanaḥ*) and related expressions (e.g., *śāśvatadharma*) are by no means foreign to traditional Hinduism. Before the encounter with the West, however, they were not used as self-descriptions of Hinduism in the face of other religions or to characterize Hinduism as *one* religious tradition among many. Instead, they characterized the 'unshakable, venerable order' and the particular rules and norms of life which have been ever valid and are hallowed by tradition. In the *Mahābhārata*, the expression 'this is a venerable rule' or 'norm' (*eṣa dharmaḥ sanātanaḥ*) often appears as a sanctioning formula intended to emphasize the obligatory nature of social and religious rules. The occurrence of this expression in the *Nārāyaṇīya* section is less exemplary; and references to the 'venerable root of the venerable dharma' (*sanātanasya dharmasya mūlam etat sanātanam*) are infrequent and somewhat atypical. Often, *sanātanadharma* and similar expressions appear in the plural. For example, the *Bhagavadgītā* refers to the 'venerable norms for the families' (*kuladharamāḥ sanātanā*). When Kṛṣṇa is described in Gītā verse XI, 18 as *śāśvatadharmagoptā sanātanaḥ,* he is not being presented as the 'defender of Hinduism,' but rather as the 'protector of the established norms.' Manu also uses *sanātanadharma* to refer to particular statutes or norms, e.g., for the king or the warrior, and even explicitly uses the plural when speaking of the unshakable (i.e., traditionally established) 'customs and statutes of the countries, castes, and families.' This use

Viṣṇudharmasūtra, Viṣṇu and other purāṇas expressly provide that one should not observe but give up what was once Dharma, if it has come to be hateful to the people and if it would end in unhappiness' (*History of Dharmaśāstra,* Vol. V, Part II (second edition), Poona: Bhandarkar Oriental Research Institute, 1977, p. 1629.

[83] Flood, Gavin, *An Introduction to Hinduism,* Cambridge: Cambridge University Press, 1996, pp. 11–12.

still largely prevailed in very late texts up to the *Mahānirvāṇatantra*. The words *vyavahāra* ('custom,' 'habitual practice') and *vidhi* ('injunction') were also occasionally associated with *sanātana*. As late as the *Śāstratattvavinirṇaya* of Nīlakaṇṭha Śāstrī Gore (1844), who later converted to Christianity, we may still as a rule find the old use or even the plural form.

When, in contrast, modern pundits describe themselves as 'members' or 'followers of the *sanātanadharma*' (*sanātanadharmīya, sanātanadharmāvalambin*), then this exemplifies a way of using *sanātanadharma* which exhibits the influence of the European concept of religion.[84]

The use of the word in the singular, however, in *epigraphic* sources, as distinguished from the literary, goes much further. As P.V. Kane points out:

One of the earliest occurrences of the word *sanātanadharma* is found in the Khanapur plates of Mādhavavarman (in E.I. Vol. 27, p. 312) edited by Dr V.V. Mirashi, who assigns it to about the 6th century A.D., in the description of the donee as *yajanayājanādhyayanādhyāpanadāna pratigrahāyā (ya?) śrutismṛtivihitasanātanadharmakarmaniratāya*, etc.' The land granted was in Returaka (modern Retrem in the Satara District of the Mahārāṣṭra State). Another early reference to the phrase *sanātana dharma* is in *Brahmapurāṇa* II.33.37–8: *adrohaścāpyalobhaśca tapo bhūtadayā damaḥ, brahmacaryaṁ tathā satyamnukroṣaḥ kṣamā dhṛtiḥ. sanātanasya dharmasya mūlametadudāhṛtam.* The words *sanātanadharma* are used in the sense of ancient practice no longer prevalent in Ādiparva 122.18 (Ch. Ed.), and in the sense of 'duty recognized long ago' in *Rāmāyaṇa, Ayodhyākāṇḍa* 19.20, 21.10 etc.[85]

2. Its modern use is criticized on slightly different grounds by Julius Lipner. He writes:

Many Hindus call themselves sanātanists, i.e., those who follow the eternal *dharma*. But we shall see that it is far from clear what this eternal *dharma* is. We have noted that Hinduism is a dynamic, living reality (or rather, a macro-reality of organically united micro-realities, analogous to an old banyan) whose strength lies in its ability to adapt to circumstances while it maintains strands of continuity with the past. But one cannot trace this continuity in an essentialist manner. It is a continuity of vital elements whose composition varies as a function of the different

[84] Halbfass, Wilhelm, *op. cit.*, p. 344.
[85] Kane, P.V., *op. cit.*, Vol. V, Part II (second edition), p. 1629, note 2612.

living centres of Hinduism which are to be found not only in the world at large but, perhaps most importantly, in India itself. These vital elements cannot be isolated as static essences. The elements composing one person's or group's eternal *dharma* may differ significantly from those of another. Yet both are Hindus. And who is to say which perception of eternal *dharma* is normative? Besides, the expression 'eternal (*sanātana*) *dharma*' seems to imply that Hinduism cannot or should not undergo change. But this is a highly contentious implication, to say the least. Where does reformed Hinduism—with which Hindu history is replete—fit in? And the multitude of little and great reformers of Hinduism, often regarded as the glory of Hindu tradition by Hindus and non-Hindus alike? It seems that to say that one is a sanātanist is more prescriptive than descriptive. It is chiefly to say what one believes Hinduism should be rather than what Hinduism is. It is to say that one does not belong to, or rather want to belong to, particular reform movements in Hinduism. (On the other hand, it may be to say that one should belong to this rather than to that reform movement, since the former has captured what the latter has not, i.e., the eternal essence of Hinduism.) It is a declaration of intent, and a rather tendentious if unclear declaration at that.[86]

3. Wilhelm Halbfass also criticizes its modern use from a different angle. He writes:

A great variety of representatives of modern Hindu thought have laid claim to the concept of *sanātanadharma*, traditional pandits as well as Vivekananda, Radhakrishnan, and other 'Neo-Hindus,' the founders and followers of reform movements as well as their orthodox opponents. A plethora of positions have been defended and propagated under this title: at first *sanātanadharma* was a concept of self-assertion against Christianity, a religion which had a temporal beginning and an historical founding figure; in this sense, *sanātanadharma* was synonymous with *vaidikadharma* and had a restorative and apologetic function. Later, the expression *sanātanadharma* increasingly became associated with such western concepts as the *philosophia perennis*, the 'universal religion' or 'eternal religion,' appearing as a program of deistic openness and a search for common denominators of all religions. Yet even in this context, *sanātanadharma* still remained a concept of self-assertion, for Hinduism alone was supposed to provide the framework for the fulfillment of the universal potential inherent in the various religions.

[86] Lipner, Julius, *Hindus: Their Religious Beliefs and Practices*, London and New York: Routledge, 1994, pp. 12–13.

Accordingly, it was not considered merely as one religion among many, but rather as a comprehensive and transcending context for these other religions.[87]

Hinduism can, however, be referred to as sanātana dharma if these semantic traps are avoided. In this acceptable sense, however, it may apply to the tradition in more than one way. In other words, the expression sanātana dharma may be understood at multiple levels in the context of modern Hinduism.

(1) One meaning of the word sanātana is immemorial. Sanātana dharma, therefore, would mean a religion that has come down to us from immemorial times. What could be the significance of such a statement?

Hinduism can be distinguished from many other religions of the world on the basis that it does not possess an individual founder. This fact possesses a comparative as well as a philosophical significance.

Its comparative significance arises from the fact that it allows the Hindu to claim that his is the original primordial religion from which the various historical religions have branched off in course of time.

The point is most easily made using India as an example. There was the original Vedic tradition, a cumulative tradition deriving from Vedic times, which continues to this day. At various points in time, however, other traditions chose to distance themselves from it. When the Buddha did so, it gave rise to Buddhism. When Mahāvira did so, Jainism appeared. When Guru Nānak did so, Sikhism appeared. Some consider it a moot point whether these historical founders were in fact breaking away from the primordial tradition, but to the extent that Buddhism, Jainism, and Sikhism consider themselves as distinct religions, they could be regarded as *historical* offshoots from the *immemorial* tradition.

The philosophical significance of the word has to do with the credibility of a tradition which looks up to a single individual, compared to one which relies on collective inspiration.

[87] Halbfass, Wilhelm, *op. cit.*, pp. 346–7.

Both the Hindu and non-Hindu communities are voluntary communities and accept the teachings of their respective 'founders.' The plurality we are concerned with here is not at the level of the followers but founders. Hinduism is founded, if we may call it that, by a class of people known as ṛṣis or seers, whereas Buddhism, Jainism, and Sikhism have been founded by individuals. Thus,

> we may take as a good example of it in Jainism, which traces its truths to the insight of great prophets like Mahāvīra. For a knowledge of the world which transcends common experience, we depend according to this view entirely upon the authority of individual insight. In this appeal to the experience of an individual, others see a risk for, in their view, nobody's private insight can carry with it the guarantee of its own validity. As Kumārila, a well-known leader of orthodox thought, has remarked in discussing a related topic, a 'vision' that has unfolded itself to but one single person, may after all be an illusion. This is not to impugn the good faith of the saint; it only means that the excellence of the character of a teacher is no guarantee of the truth of his teaching. To avoid this possible defect of subjectivity orthodox thinkers postulate in the place of testimony, based upon the intuition of a single sage, another, viz. *śruti* or 'revelation'—otherwise known as the Veda which, it is claimed, will not mislead us since it has emanated from God or is supernatural in some other sense. As commonly explained, the *śruti* is tradition which is looked upon as immemorial (*sanātana*) in its character because its origin cannot be traced to any mortal being.[88]

The point needs to be refined in view of the fact that the followers of these religions other than Hinduism regard these religions as founded by a series of 'prophets'. Thus, Buddhism speaks of past (and future) Buddhas, Jainism of past (and future) Tīrthaṅkaras, and Sikhism of a succession of Gurus beginning with Guru Nānak (1469–1539) and ending with Guru Gobind Singh (1666–1708), who installed the Guru Granth Sāhib as the authority for the Sikhs after him. The issue is therefore not one merely of plurality of founders, as the successive Buddhas, Tirthaṅkaras, or Gurus could be looked upon as founders. The question is an epistemological

[88] Hiriyanna, M., *The Essentials of Indian Philosophy*, London: Allen & Unwin, 1949, pp. 44–5.

one and has to do with singularity or plurality as a founding principle.

Thus the standard here becomes eventually a society of men, and not an individual; and, by virtue of the objective status which it thus acquires, its deliverances are taken to possess an authority which cannot belong to those of anybody's private intuition. Herein may be said to lie the superiority of *śruti* to mere *smṛti,* in the sense given to it above. The Mīmāṁsā and the Vedānta are the systems that accept 'revelation,' in this sense, as the means to a knowledge of supersensuous truth.[89]

(2) Sanātana can also mean *old,* but one needs to be careful here—many points are involved. The first of these has to do with the distinction we draw between the 'old' and the 'new', on the assumption that what was applicable at one time is not applicable for another. This idea needs to be revisited, but does not deny the validity of the distinction. The criterion has to do with *applicability,* rather than *antiquity.* Slavery may have been practiced for ages, but is now adjudged universally as inappropriate—and therefore inapplicable to our times. Nor is this point related to the fact expressed so well in the saying that the more things change, the more they remain the same. For, if all change is superficial in this sense, then ancient principles possess an abiding relevance. That is not the point. We may underestimate the persistence of evil, but that recognition does not render it any less evil; it has to be removed. It is not along these lines that I wish to develop this point.

The direction in which I wish to progress upon is the following: One could begin by distinguishing between religion and ideology in the following manner—that while ideology offers *contemporary answers* to the *perennial problems* of society and polity, it could be argued that, by contrast, religion offers *perennial solutions* to our *contemporary problems.* The suggestion that the Islamic *sharī'ah* provides a blueprint for solving modern economic and social problems is a good example of this attitude. I do not wish to comment on this example further, but would like to say a few more words about the underlying attitude involved here.

[89] *Ibid.*, p. 45.

If we then look at religion in this light, then the word sanātana can take on another sense—something akin to so old that it is new. The reader is doubtless familiar with the word *purāṇa,* as in the eighteen Purāṇas. There is a traditional gloss of this word, probably etymologically indefensible from a modern point of view, but enormously suggestive from a traditional hermeneutical perspective—*purā api navam,* that is to say, new despite being old. There is the hint here that a religious tradition may possess such vitality as places it beyond the reach of such distinctions as 'tradition' and 'modernity'.

The startling example here is provided by yoga. Yoga is one of the most ancient dimensions of the Hindu tradition, and its origins have been traced back at least to about 3000 B.C., or at least to the mature phase of the Harappan period. In the famous proto-Śiva seals, for instance, 'the deity is sitting cross-legged in a *padmāsana* posture with his eyes turned towards the tip of the nose, which evidences the Yogīśvara aspect of the deity.'[90] Even if this involves some measure of overinterpretation, it is hard to deny the prevalence of some form of yoga in Harappan culture. This aspect of the latter becomes particularly interesting when we correlate it with another of its facets—its uniformity. A modern historian has drawn attention to the point:

Of unremarkable profile, then, the mud-and-rubble mounds of the Harappan cities and settlements nevertheless made an impression on Bhandarkar's successors in the Archaeological Survey. Happily ignoring his report, R.D. Banerji and Sir John Marshall resumed explorations at Mohenjo-daro in the late 1920s. Ernest Mackay and Sir Mortimer Wheeler continued their work and also re-examined Harappa, a collection of mounds in the Panjab whence in the nineteenth century bricks similar to those at Mohenjo-daro had been removed by the wagonload as ballast for a 160-kilometre section of the Lahore-Multan railway line. After Independence and the Partition of the Subcontinent in 1947, B.B. Lal, J.P. Joshi, S.R. Rao, M. Rafique Mughal, and a host

[90] Pusalkar, A.D., 'The Indus Valley Civilization', in *The Vedic Age*, R.C. Majumdar (ed.), London: George Allen & Unwin Ltd., 1952, p. 187.

of others extended operations to numerous other sites with outstanding results. What amazed all these pioneers, and what remains the distinctive characteristic of the several hundred Harrappan sites now known, is their apparent similarity: 'Our overwhelming impression is of cultural uniformity, both throughout the several centuries during which the Harappan civilization flourished, and over the vast area it occupied.'[91]

Are the homogenizing—not to say hegemonizing—impulses of modern Western civilization and of globalization to be related to the current tsunami of interest in yoga?

(3) Another meaning of the word sanātana identifies it with the imperishable. Hence, a religion that sets an imperishable example could also be called sanātana dharma. Mahatma Gandhi provided intimations of such a meaning when asked whether he would allow a whole people to perish while offering non-violent resistance. He replied that although these people may perish, they will set an *imperishable* example which will shine forever. The use of the word *sanātana*, at its loftiest, could point to this paradoxical possibility.

(4) A fourth interpretation of the word sanātana, when taken as meaning 'eternal', can also indicate the eternality of potentiality.[92] This conceptualization is helpful in drawing attention to the fact that 'to define Hinduism is to deny the Hindu the right to freedom and integrity of his faith. What he may do tomorrow, no man can say today.'[93]

(5) Yet, another rendering of sanātana, when understood as 'eternal', could yield the following: It is the eternal religion of which the various so-called 'religions' are parts. The word

[91] Kerry, John, *India: A History*, New York: Atlantic Monthly Press, 2000, p. 9.

[92] In *Sāṁkhya*, for instance, '*Prakṛti*, 'matter,' is not an object of physics but metaphysics. Its eternity is not the nondestructibility of a concrete object but of potentiality' (Klaus K. Klostermaier, *A Survey of Hinduism* (second edition), Albany, N.Y.: State University of New York Press, 1994, p. 407.

[93] Smith, Wilfred Cantwell, *The Meaning and End of Religion*, New York: The Macmillan Company, 1963, p. 145.

'eternal' here takes on the sense of the eternal archetype, as it were. Now,

The traditional relationship of the 'totality' of Hinduism to the Hindu sects became the model for the relationship between Hinduism and the world's religions: 'Hinduism has evolved out of itself a multitude of *religions*, each of which bears perfect analogy to Christianity and Mohammedanism so far as the application of this term is concerned.... We commit an obvious logical fallacy when we put Hinduism by the side of Christianity, Mohammedanism, Buddhism, etc., to signify that it is one of the sectarian religions of the world.'

The harmonizing and 'spiritualizing' of sects and local cults by including them in the 'unity' of Hinduism or by subordinating them to its highest stages, the Vedānta, was considered to be the prototype and basis for a global harmonizing. Radhakrishnan spoke of the acceptance and neutralization of local Indian cults within Hinduism, adding: 'Hinduism is not limited in scope to the geographical area which is described as India.... There is nothing which prevents it from extending to the uttermost parts of the world.'[94]

This sense of sanātana dharma as a description of Hinduism becomes particularly significant when Hinduism is understood more as a philosophy or form of wisdom than as a religion in the creedal sense of the term.[95]

(6) A final stance in which Hinduism would be called sanātana dharma may initially come as a surprise, but relates to the 'very basic fact of internal plurality and *perennial* dissent'[96] as diagnostic features of Hinduism. In this sense, Hinduism is the religion of perpetual dissent—or at least debate. Surprising support for such an interpretation is provided by the following remarks of Irfan Habib:

There were the religious traditions coming from ancient India, which by Mughal times began to be described under the term 'Hindu.' The author of *Dabistan-i-Mazahib* is hard put to describe what the beliefs of a Hindu are and ultimately he takes shelter in a very convenient position

[94] Halbfass, Wilhelm, *op. cit.*, pp. 346–7.

[95] Renou, Louis (ed.), *Hinduism*, New York: George Braziller, 1962, pp. 56–7.

[96] Menski, Werner F., *Hindu Law: Beyond Tradition and Modernity*, New Delhi: Oxford University Press, 2003, p. 5, note 7, emphasis supplied.

but the only possible position—Hindus are those who have been arguing with each other within the same framework of argument over the centuries. If they recognize each other as persons whom we can either support or oppose in a religious argument, then both parties are Hindus. The Jains, although they rejected Brahmanism, were still Hindus because they were arguing and polemicising with Brahmins. Such arguments were not taking place between Hindus and Muslims. The Muslims did not share any basic terminology with the others. Muslims had their own framework, an ideological framework, the semitic framework. . . .[97]

[97] Cited in Shashi Joshi and Bhagwan Josh, *Struggle for Hegemony in India 1920–47,* New Delhi: Sage Publications, 1994, p. 185.

XIV

Māyā

Māyā is the word most often invoked in modern Hinduism, along with the concept it embodies, to explain the relationship of the universe to the ultimate reality, whether defined absolutistically or theistically.

Although the word is classical, in modern Hinduism it receives certain distinct emphases. One sense in which it has been used is to indicate the sense of mystery involved in this relationship. This recognition of the sense of mystery conveyed by it is relatively new in its emphasis. In earlier times, the word was often used as an explanation of the relationship; it is now as often used in recognition of the fact that this relationship cannot be explained, or at least adequately explained. This is true even when the word is taken as suggestive of illusionism, an association from which modern Hinduism recoils.[98] That

[98] See Satischandra Chatterjee and Dhirendramohan Datta, *An Introduction to Indian Philosophy*, University of Calcutta, 1968, p. 416: 'Māyā, as well as every illusory object, is said to be indescribable owing to a genuine difficulty. In so far as it *appears to be* something, an illusion or illusory object cannot be said to be unreal like a square circle or the son of a barren woman which never even appears to exist. Again in so far as it is sublated or contradicted afterwards by some experience, it cannot be said to be absolutely real like Ātman or Brahman whose reality is never contradicted. Māyā and every illusory object have this nature and compel us to recognize this nature as something unique and indescribable in terms of ordinary

one thing should appear as something which it is not is indeed mysterious, and this is clearly recognized in the agnosticism that characterizes the discussions of the relationship between Reality and the world. S. Radhakrishnan writes:

> The history of philosophy in India as well as Europe has been one long illustration of the inability of the human mind to solve the mystery of the relation of God to the world. The greatest thinkers are those who admit the mystery and comfort themselves by the idea that the human mind is not omniscient. Śaṁkara in the East and Bradley in the West adopt this wise attitude of agnosticism. We have the universe with its distinctions. It is not self-sufficient. It rests on something else, and that is the Absolute. The relation between the two is a mystery.[99]

The same point was made more directly by Swami Vivekananda in the paper he read at the World Parliament of Religions in Chicago in 1893:

> Why should the free, perfect, and pure being be thus under the thralldom of matter, is the next question. How can the perfect soul be deluded into the belief that it is imperfect? We have been told that the Hindus shirk the question and say that no such question can be there. Some thinkers want to answer it by positing one or more quasi-perfect beings, and use big scientific names to fill up the gap. But naming is not explaining. The question remains the same. How can the perfect become the quasi-perfect; how can the pure, the absolute, change even a microscopic particle of its nature? But the Hindu is sincere. He does not want to take shelter under sophistry. He is brave enough to face the question in a manly fashion; and his answer is: 'I do not know. I do not know how the perfect being, the soul, came to think of itself as imperfect, as joined to and conditioned by matter.' But the fact is a fact for all that. It is a fact in everybody's consciousness that one thinks of oneself as the body. The Hindu does not attempt to explain why one thinks one is the body. The answer that it is the will of God is no

---

reality or unreality. To say that māyā is indescribable is only to describe a fact, namely our *inability* to bring it under any ordinary category, and it does not mean any violation of the law of contradiction. In fact, as "real" means here the "absolutely real" and "unreal" "the absolutely unreal," they do not constitute a pair of contradictories any more than two words like "extremely cold" and "extremely hot" do.'

[99] Radhakrishnan, S., *The Hindu View of Life*, pp. 67–8.

explanation. This is nothing more than what the Hindu says, 'I do not know.'[100]

In the context of Śaṅkara's philosophy, the view has often been expressed by his critics—in both classical and modern India as well as in the West—that the doctrine of māyā, to which he largely gave currency, reduced the ontological status of the world virtually to that of an illusion—with dire practical consequences. This interpretation has been vigorously contested by modern Hindu scholars and saints in both its absolutistic and theistic version. S. Radhakrishnan comments that 'It is not fair to represent Śaṅkara's view as an illusionist.' In fact, Śaṅkara repudiates 'subjectivism', and 'affirms the extra-mental reality of objects'.[101] In Śaṅkara's system, transcendental idealism is consistent with empirical realism, which answers the question as to why, upon realization, the universe does not disappear like an illusion: 'When the illusion of the mirage is dissipated by scientific knowledge, the illusion stands there though it is no longer able to tempt us. The world is not so much denied as reinterpreted.'[102]

Another consequence that is said to result from the misreading of Śaṅkara's doctrine of māyā is the devaluation of the world and a consequent indifference to the sufferings of others. This is strongly contested in modern Hinduism by both theists and absolutists. Mahatma Gandhi writes under the rubric of māyā: 'Joy or what men call happiness may be, as it really is, a dream in a fleeting and transitory world, where everything is like a dissolving phantasmagoria. But we cannot dismiss the suffering of our fellow creatures as unreal and thereby provide a moral alibi for ourselves. Even dreams are true while they last, and to the sufferer his suffering is a grim reality. Anyway, whether the world be real or unreal, we have

[100] *The Complete Works of Swami Vivekananda*, Vol. I, (Mayavati Memorial Edition), Calcutta: Advaita Ashram, 1986, pp. 9–10.

[101] Radhakrishnan, S., *The Hindu View of Life*, p. 65.

[102] *Ibid.*, pp. 65–6. Ramaṇa Maharṣi similarly states that the world 'is seen by both the ignorant and the realized'...'but their viewpoints differ' (Joe and Guinevere Miller, *op. cit.*, p. 85.).

certain duties in life which must be faced, understood and duly performed while we are in this world.'[103] The threads of this position in an absolutistic context are on display in full colour in the following passage from Ramaṇa Maharṣi, whose perspicacity makes up for its length. When asked whether the universe is a dream, he said:

From the point of view of *jnana* or the reality, the pain you speak of is certainly a dream, as is the world of which the pain is an infinitesimal part. In the dream also you yourself feel hunger. You see others suffering hunger. You feed yourself and, moved by pity, feed the others that you find suffering from hunger. So long as the dream lasts, all those hunger pains are quite as real as you now think the pain you see in the world to be. It is only when you wake up that you discover that the pain in the dream was unreal. You might have eaten to the full and gone to sleep. You dream that you work hard and long in the hot sun all day, are tired and hungry and want to eat a lot. Then you get up and find your stomach is full and you have not stirred out of your bed. But all this is not to say that while you are in the dream you can act as if the pain you feel there is not real. The hunger in the dream has to be assuaged by the food in the dream. The fellow beings you found so hungry in the dream had to be provided with food in that dream. You can never mix up the two states, the dream and the waking state. Till you reach the state of *jnana* and thus wake out of this *maya*, you must do social service by relieving suffering whenever you see it. But even then you must do it, as we are told, without *ahamkara*, that is without the sense 'I am the doer', but feeling, 'I am the Lord's tool.' Similarly one must not be conceited and think, 'I am helping a man below me He needs help. I am in a position to help. I am superior and he inferior.' You must help the man as a means of worshipping God in that man. All such service too is for you the Self, not for anybody else. You are not helping anybody else, but only yourself.[104]

While Ramaṇa Maharṣi seems to maintain here that one must serve the world selflessly despite the fact that it may be māyā or like a dream or illusion at least from the standpoint of the *jñānī*, S. Radhakrishnan argues that such is not even the case. He is not prepared to make the concession

[103] M.K. Gandhi, *Hindu Dharma*, p. 47.

[104] Godman, David (ed.), *The Teachings of Sri Ramana Maharishi*, London and New York: Arkana, 1985, p. 212.

Ramaṇa Maharṣi seems to make. Ishwar C. Harris carefully notes that

Radhakrishnan's discussion of *Māyā* is spread over many of his writings. At different occasions he gives various views denoted by the concept of *Māyā*. Sometimes he views *Māyā* as a creative power of Brahman. At another occasion it is viewed as *līlā* or the play of God. It is the creation out of the abundance of God's Joy. Elsewhere it is interpreted as mystery. It is also seen as ignorance or *avidyā* which asserts that the real nature of the world is hidden from man. *However, nowhere does he ever look at the concept of Māyā to denote 'illusion'*. What is significant from the standpoint of the issue of unity being discussed here is the fact that Radhakrishnan maintains the unity of all particulars into one Universal Absolute. This is the monistic vision of the Vedānta philosophy which provides the basis for his universalism. The world (*Māyā*) and Brahman are ultimately united. This union explains the very nature of reality itself. According to Radhakrishnan, failure to comprehend this unity results in the belief that *Māyā* is illusion.[105]

In scrupulously avoiding the doctrine of māyā to be tainted by illusionism, Radhakrishnan reflects an essential aspect of the modern understanding of it. And this is done while retaining the classical link of the doctrine with Śaṅkara. This point is also presented with both brevity and clarity by Ramaṇa Maharṣi as follows:

D.: When the Upanishads say that all is Brahman, how can we agree with Shankara that this world is illusory?

B.: Shankara also said that this world is Brahman or the Self. What he objected to is one's imagining that the Self is limited by the names and forms that constitute the world. He only said that the world has no reality apart from Brahman. Brahman or the Self is like a cinema screen and the world like the pictures on it. You can see the picture only so long as there is a screen. But when the observer himself becomes the screen only the Self remains.

Shankara has been criticized for his philosophy of Maya (illusion) without understanding his meaning. He made three statements: that Brahman is real, that the universe is unreal, and that Brahman is the Universe. He did not stop with the second. The third statement explains

[105] Harris, Ishwar C., *Radhakrishnan: The Profile of a Universalist*, Calcutta: Minerva Associates [Publications] Pvt. Ltd., 1982, p. 120, emphasis added.

the first two; it signifies that when the Universe is perceived apart from Brahman, that perception is false and illusory. What it amounts to is that phenomena are real when experienced as the Self and illusory when seen apart from the Self.

The Self alone exists and is real. The world, the individual and God are, like the illusory appearance of silver in the mother-of-pearl, imaginary creations of the Self. They appear and disappear simultaneously. Actually, the Self alone is the world, the 'I' and God. All that exists is only a manifestation of the Supreme.

D.: What is reality?

B.: Reality must always be real. It has no names or forms but is what underlies them. It underlies all limitations, being itself limitless. It is not bound in any way. It underlies unrealities, being itself Real. It is that which is. It is as it is. It transcends speech and is beyond description such as being or non-being.[106]

The saint ultimately supports the scholar.

[106] Osborne, Arthur (ed.), *The Teachings of Bhagavan Sri Ramana Maharshi in His Own Words,* Tiruvannamalai: Sri Ramanaramam, 1971, pp. 11–12. D = devotee; B = Bhagavan Ramaṇa.

XV

Mokṣa

The concept of mokṣa in classical Hinduism is said to be essentially one of individual liberation. It is the individual jīva who transcends māyā and passes beyond the realm of saṁsāra, beyond the pale of rebirth either in a theistic or an absolutistic manner. Just as single stars may fall but the firmament remains in place, individual jīvas could attain mokṣa leaving the saṁsāra in place. Some exceptions were hinted at—exceptional souls, even after liberation, sometimes decide to return, not as reincarnations, but rather as incarnations to help others along. However, the standard, if not dominant note, was set by the refrain that one is born alone, bound alone, dies alone, and is liberated alone.

The concept of mokṣa, as it has evolved in modern Hinduism, tends to be less self-centred. To begin with, the more communal dimension of liberation, such as exists in classical Hinduism, has been recognized, and even emphasized. There is the case of Prahlāda who 'criticises those performers of penance in the forests who strive for their own salvation indifferent to the suffering of the erring mortals and he says that he does not desire his own salvation unless these erring people are taken along' in a hymn in the *Bhāgavata Purāṇa.*[107]

[107] Radhakrishnan, S. (tr.), *The Brahma Sūtra: The Philosophy of Spiritual Life*, p. 214.

Moreover, the world is redeemable, for otherwise, as Śaṅkara says, 'the first released person would have destroyed the world once for all'.[108] To the extent that many schools of Hindu thought believe in living liberation, such a person spontaneously acts for the good of all, 'like the spring season', combining absolutism with altruism. Theistic Hinduism is characterized by communion with God, and the way leading to such communion is itself characterized by the communion of the devotees (*satsaṅga*). In some accounts, the lovers of God are teleported en masse from earth to heaven along with God. Thus, when 'In the Viṣṇupurāṇa the world *anurāga* is used for "bhakti", after describing the ascent of Rama and his brothers to heaven, it says that the people of the capital of Kosala—who had deep affection for those incarnate parts of the Bhagavān (Viṣṇu), having their minds fixed on them—reached the position of residence in the same world with them.'[109] The path of action involves not only doing one's duty, but also helping others (*lokasaṅgraha*). Examples of such modern altruistic takes on classical concepts of liberation, in Hinduism, can be multiplied. The Advaitin Appaya Dīkṣita, for instance, proffers this remarkable view in his famous compendium—the *Siddhanta-Leśa-Saṅgraha*:

> Liberation being the manifestation of our nature and nothing adventitious, cannot be denied to or withheld from anyone. Universal liberation is more than a possibility; it is a logical necessity. Different souls will require a long or short period of time in proportion to their capacity to get rid of *avidyā* but its final removal is certain. So long as there is a single unrealised soul, *māyā* is not completely destroyed and there can be no absolute realization for any other soul, however advanced it may be in the path of perfection.[110]

[108] *Ibid.*, p. 208.

[109] Kane, P.V., *History of Dharmaśāstra*, Vol. V, Part II, p. 959.

[110] Radhakrishnan, S. (tr.), *op. cit.*, p. 211. This hints at the doctrine of *sarvamukti*—that the liberation of one involves the liberation of all. It is worth noting that this statement about the liberation of one involving the liberation of all can be understood in divergent ways. One could argue that if one is liberated, all are liberated, as when if one person awakes all the persons in that persons' dream disappear. One could also argue, and this

What was latent in classical Hinduism has become patent in modern Hinduism—in both its theistic and absolutistic versions. The theistic version is presented with sublime passion by Mahatma Gandhi, who declares: 'My uniform experience has convinced me that there is no other God than truth'[111], and then goes on to say:

To see the universal and all-pervading Spirit of Truth face to face one must be able to love the meanest of creation as oneself. And a man who aspires after that cannot afford to keep out of any field of life. That is why my devotion to Truth has drawn me into the field of politics; and I can say without the slightest hesitation, and yet in all humility, that those who say that religion has nothing to do with politics do not know what religion means.

Identification with everything that lives is impossible without self-purification; without self-purification the observance of the law of Ahimsa must remain an empty dream; God can never be realized by one who is not pure of heart. Self-purification therefore must mean purification in all the walks of life. And purification being highly infectious, purification of oneself necessarily leads to the purification of one's surrounding.[112]

But what is all this for? Mahatma Gandhi states the reason with surprising directness: 'What I want to achieve—what I have been striving and planning to achieve these thirty years—is self-realization, to see God face to face, to attain moksa.'[113]

S. Radhakrishnan also seeks to make the absolutistic concept of liberation more comprehensive by contrasting Advaitic conceptions with those of Sāṅkhya, when he writes:

There are Advaitins who argue that each soul is an individual existence trying to get away from its own self-deceiving. They insist on the necessity for individual salvation and this has little to do with the destiny of the cosmos or other souls. Such a view is more in accordance

---

seems to be the intended meaning here, that none *in* the dream can be liberated, unless all in the dream are liberated.

[111] *Gandhi's Autobiography: The Story of My Experiments with Truth,* Mahadev Desai (tr.), Washington, D.C.: Public Affairs Press, 1948, p. 615.

[112] *Ibid.*, pp. 615–16.

[113] *Ibid.*, pp. 4–5.

with the *Sāṁkhya* theory of a plurality of spirits (*puruṣa*) for in it each spirit is a separate eternal entity which falls into subjection to *prakṛti* (nature) and pursues its separate cycle of cosmic existence and works for its separate release. The *Sāṁkhya* theory affirms a dualism between spirit and nature and we cannot be certain that the free spirit that has once fallen into subjection by the disturbance of the equilibrium will not again fall into subjection by a repetition of the disturbance. According to the *Advaita Vedānta*, in each soul separately the one spirit has assumed the form of individual being. If it gets rid of the deception it may be saved, but the continuance of the self-deception in myriads of other souls will make for the time process. If the spirit is eternally free in itself and is also bound in the cosmos, it is not enough for a few souls to release themselves from time to time out of this deception.[114]

The most innovative move in this direction, however, comes from Aurobindo Ghose, involving a change both in direction and design. 'In the past, saints and sages have risen from the lower level to the higher. But they did not attempt, says Śrī Aurobindo, to bring the supermind down into the consciousness of the earth and make it fixed there. "This is what the successful yogis of the future must strive for." The ideal of divine humanity will then be accomplished, and the world will be transformed into the kingdom of God.'[115]

It is not surprising that concepts of mokṣa should differ in modern Hinduism. They also differed within classical Hinduism, which not only embraced various 'stages of mukti—viz. *sālokya* (place in the Lord's world), *sāmīpya* (proximity), *sārūpya* (attaining the same form as God), and *sāyujya* (absorption)'[116]—but also consisted of different conceptualization of the stages themselves. According to Madhva's school, for instance:

The state of liberation is of four kinds *sālokya, sāmīpya, sārūpya* and *sāyujya. Sāyujya* is the entrance of the freed souls into the body of God where they share in the enjoyment of God in his own body. Only

[114] Radhakrishnan, S. (tr.), *The Brahma Sūtra: The Philosophy of Spiritual Life*, p. 223.

[115] Mahadevan, T.M.P., *Outlines of Hinduism*, pp. 238–9.

[116] Kane, P.V., *History of Dharmaśāstra*, Vol. V, Part II, p. 1631.

deities have this kind of liberation. They can at will come out of God and remain separate from him. *Sālokya* is residence in heaven where the freed souls have the satisfaction of the continual sight of God. *Sāmīpya* is continual residence near God as enjoyed by the sages. *Sārūpya* is enjoyed by God's attendants who have outward forms similar to those which God possesses. The freed souls are different from one another.[117]

[117] Radhakrishnan, S. (tr.), *The Brahma Sūtra: The Philosophy of Spiritual Life*, pp. 65–6.

XVI

Jñāna Yoga

Hinduism is indebted to Ramaṇa Maharṣi (1879–1950) for simplifying the path of knowledge in modern times. This point can be made by taking another look at the *locus classicus* of the path of knowledge in classical Hinduism, namely, *Bṛhadāraṇyaka Upaniṣad* (IV.5.6): *Ātmā va are draṣṭavyaḥ śrotavyo mantavyo nididhyāsitavyaḥ*—'Verity the Self is to be seen, to be heard, to be reflected on, to be meditated upon.'

According to the classical Hindu understanding of this passage, the various stages of self-realization through the path of knowledge are spelled out here. According to the Bhāmatī school of Advaita Vedānta, this involves three stages: (1) audition, (2) reflection, and (3) meditation. According to the Vivaraṇa school, the first stage—that of audition—suffices to trigger realization in the absence of inhibiting factors.[118]

If one examines the method proposed by Ramaṇa Maharṣi, it is possible to argue that, according to him, the passage can be contracted thus: 'To be seen', or *draṣṭavaḥ* alone. *See* who you are. If you look deeply into yourself you will find that you identify yourself with the ego that is really non-existent!

[118] See P.S. Roodurmun, *Bhāmatī and Vivaraṇa Schools of Advaita Vedānta: A Critical Approach*, Delhi: Motilal Banarsidass, 2002.

The process may be described in more detail, beginning with the seeker asking the question: *Who am I?*

When thoughts arise during the meditation one is not to follow them up but to watch them and ask: 'What is this thought? Where did it come from? And to whom? To me—and who am I?' So each thought disappears when scrutinized and is turned back to the basic I-thought. If impure thoughts rise up they are to be treated in the same way, for *sadhana* really does what psycho-analysis claims to do—it clears out the filth from the subconscious, brings it up to the light of day and destroys it. 'Yes, all kinds of thoughts arise in meditation. That is only right, for what lies hidden in you is brought out. Unless it rises up how can it be destroyed?' (*Maharshi's Gospel.*)

All thought-forms are alien to this mode of meditation. Sometimes a devotee would ask Sri Bhagavan if he could use a theme such as 'I am He,' or any other, during the enquiry but he always forbade it. On one occasion when a devotee had suggested one theme after another, he explained: 'All thoughts are inconsistent with Realization. The right thing to do is to exclude thoughts of oneself and all other thoughts. Thought is one thing and Realization is quite another.'

Arthur Osborne goes on to explain that:

There is no answer to the Who-am-I question. There can be no answer for it is dissolving the I-thought, which is the parent of all other thoughts, and piercing beyond to the stillness where thought is not. 'Suggestive replies to the enquiry, such as "Sivoham" (I am Siva) are not to be given to the mind during meditation. The true answer will come of itself. No answer the ego can give can be right.' The answer is the awakening current of awareness... vibrating as the very essence of one's being and yet impersonal. By constant practice this is to be made more and more frequent until it becomes continuous, not only during meditation but underlying speech and action also. Even then the *vichara* is still to be used, for the ego will try to make a truce with the current of awareness and if it is once tolerated it will gradually grow to power and then fight to recover supremacy, like the Gentiles whom the Hebrews allowed to remain in the Promised Land. Sri Bhagavan insisted (for instance, in his replies to Sivaprakasam Pillai) that the enquiry is to be kept up to the very end. Whatever states, whatever powers, whatever perceptions or visions may come, there is always the question to whom they come until the Self alone remains.[119]

[119] Osborne, Arthur, *Ramana Maharshi and the Path of Self-Knowledge*, York Beach, Maine: Samuel Weiser, Inc. 1995, pp. 151–2.

XVII

Bhakti Yoga

A characteristic of modern Hinduism is the simplification of the various yogas that lead to spiritual realization, and the recognition of their interconnection. One may first point to a case in which intense yearning or devotion to God *by itself* suffices.

Ah, that restlessness is the whole thing. Whatever path you follow—whether you are a Hindu, a Mussalmān, a Christian, a Śākta, a Vaishnava, or a Brāhmo—the vital point is restlessness. God is our Inner Guide. It doesn't matter if you take a wrong path—only you must be restless for Him. He Himself will put you on the right path.

Besides, there are errors in all paths. Everyone thinks his watch is right; but as a matter of fact no watch is absolutely right. But that doesn't hamper one's work. If a man is restless for God he gains the company of sādhus' help.[120]

The restlessness Rāmakṛṣṇa is referring to is the yearning for God.

One must have for God the yearning of a child. The Child sees nothing but confusion when his mother is away. You may try to cajole him by putting a sweetmeat in his hand; but he will not be fooled. He only says, 'No, I want to go to my mother.' One must feel such yearning for God.

[120] Swami Nikhilananda (tr.), *The Gospel of Sri Ramakrishna*, New York: Ramakrishna-Vivekananda Center, 1952, p. 673.

Ah, what yearning! How restless a child feels for his mother! Nothing can make him forget his mother. He to whom the enjoyment of worldly happiness appears tasteless, he who takes no delight in anything of the world—money, name, creature comforts, sense pleasure—, becomes sincerely grief-stricken for the vision of the Mother. And to him alone the Mother comes running, leaving all her other duties.[121]

The combination of bhakti and karma is equally effective, if we are to believe Rajagopalachari's account of Mahatma Gandhi's secret of success. He writes:

The practice of doing our work with devotion to God will give us great joy. It will give us skill and zest in our work. I can affirm without a doubt that this was the secret of Mahatma Gandhi's success. In everything that he did, in every plan that he made, in every step that he took he carried in his heart the thought of God which ever went with him as a man's shadow goes with him when he walks. This thought never hindered his work. On the contrary, it was the source of his success. In all the little tasks that we do, this thought of God will likewise stand by us like a shadow and help us in silence. It is essential for a servant of society to labour with the thought of God unceasingly in one's mind. It is as indispensable to effective work as asepsis to surgery. A pure mind is a great asset and an unfailing *sadhana.* Devotion is the only way to get it.[122]

The combination of bhakti and jñāna is also as simple as it is potent, and they may also interpenetrate. Here, the devotee begins by asking a question on devotion to the master, who in this case is Ramaṇa Maharṣi:

D.: *Śrī Bhāgavata* outlines a way to find Krishna in the Heart by prostrating to all and looking on all as the Lord Himself. Is this the right path leading to Self-realization? Is it not easier thus to adore Bhagavan in whatever meets the 'mind' than to seek the Supramental through the mental inquiry 'Who am I'?

M.: Yes, when you see God in all, do you think of God or do you not? You must certainly think of God for seeing God all around you. Keeping God in your mind becomes *dhyāna,* and *dhyāna* is the stage before

[121] *Ibid.*

[122] Rajgopalachari, C., *Sri Ramakrishna Upaniṣad,* Madras: Sri Ramakrishna Math, 1964, pp. 55–6.

Realization. Realization can only be in and of the Self. It can never be apart from the Self, and *dhyāna* must precede it. Whether you make *dhyāna* on God or on the Self, it is immaterial; for the goal is the same. You cannot by any means escape the Self. You want to see God in all, but not in yourself? If *all* is God, are you not included in that *all*? Being God yourself, is it a wonder that *all* is God? This is the method advised in *Śrī Bhāgavata* and elsewhere by others. But even for this practice there must be the seer or thinker. Who is he?

D.: How to see God, Who is all-pervasive?

M.: To see God is to *be* God. There is no 'all' apart from God for Him to pervade. He alone *is*.

D.: Should we read the *Gītā* now and then?

M.: Always.[123]

The devotee then proceeds to ask questions on first, the relationship of bhakti and jñāna; second, about his problems in pursuing devotional practices steadily, and third, once again on the relationship of bhakti and jñāna.

D.: What is the relation between *jñāna* and *bhakti*?

M.: The eternal, unbroken, natural state of abiding in the Self is *jñāna*. To abide in the Self you must love the Self. Since God is verily the Self, love of the Self is love of God; and that is *Bhakti*. *Jñāna* and *bhakti* are thus one and the same.

D.: While making *nāma-japa* for an hour or more I fall into a state like sleep. On waking up I recollect that my *japa* has been interrupted, so I try again.

M.: 'Like sleep,' that is right. It is the natural state. Because you are now associated with the ego, you consider that the natural state is something which interrupts your work. So you must have the experience repeated until you realize that it is your natural state. You will then find that *japa* is extraneous, but still it will go on automatically. Your present doubt is due to that false identity, namely of identifying yourself with the mind that does the *japa*. *Japa* means clinging to one thought to the exclusion of all other thoughts. That is its purpose. It leads to *dhyāna*, which ends in Self-realization or *jñāna*.

[123] Miller, Joe & Guinevere, *The Spiritual Teachings of Ramana Maharshi*, Boston & London: Shambhala, 1988, p. 55.

D.: How should I carry on *nāma-japa*?

M.: One should not use the Name of God mechanically and superficially without the feeling of devotion. To use the Name of God one must call upon Him with yearning and unreservedly surrender oneself to Him. Only after such surrender is the name of God constantly with the man.

D.: Where, then, is the need for inquiry or *vichāra*?

M.: Surrender can take effect only when it is done with full knowledge as to what real surrender means. Such knowledge comes after inquiry and reflection and ends invariably in self-surrender. There is no difference between *jñāna* and absolute surrender to the Lord, that is, in thought, word, and deed. To be complete, surrender must be unquestioning; the devotee cannot bargain with the Lord or demand favors at His hands. Such entire surrender comprises all: it is *jñāna* and *vairāgya*, Devotion and Love.[124]

[124] *Ibid.*, pp. 55–6.

XVIII

Karma Yoga

Karma yoga is best explained with the help of the Bhagavadgītā. The issue may be phrased as follows: As we must act in the world, how may one act to attain mokṣa? An immediate answer would be that one should give up egocentric action—for egocentricism generates karma. Here, however, a paradox is involved: If one consciously acts to give up ego-actions, then that act in itself strengthens it. Therefore, the way to get away from the ego is to perform action for its own sake, not even for the sake of getting rid of the ego. If, however, 'the notion of duty is entirely separated from its consequences' in this way, what is likely to happen?

Contrary to our fear that things might collapse, they may proceed rather smoothly, for both oneself and for society. As one is doing duty for duty's, not ego's sake, the karmic trap is being avoided. On the other hand, how does one determine what one's duty is? It is determined by one's station in life. The end result, therefore, is that both personal and social ends are reconciled and secured.

One may point out, however, that 'disinterested activity, in the literal sense of the word, is a psychological impossibility.' In that case karma could be combined with jñāna, and action performed for 'cleansing the heart' (*sattva-śuddhi*).

Alternatively, karma could be combined with bhakti, by dedicating all action to God (*īśvarārtha*).[125]

One question, however, remains. Can karma *by itself* result in mokṣa? According to the modern saint, Ānandamayī Mā (1896–1982), this too might be possible. Her position on this unexplored point deserves to be cited *in extenso.*[126]

Very well, now listen to something else. There is a stage where working is very delightful and gives intense happiness. Here one is quite unconcerned with what may or may not result from one's action; the work is done entirely for its own sake, for the love of it. Neither is there an external Guru in this, nor the love of Him. A state of being of this kind does exist. There is great diversity in the realm of action.

The sense of contentment experienced at the fulfillment of some worldly desire is relative happiness. This desire may be for one's wife, son, a relation, or any other person, and accordingly the fruit inherent in each particular action will be reaped. This is working for the sake of self-satisfaction (*bhoga*), not for the sake of union (*yoga*); it brings sorrow along with joy.

Now to come back to what has just been said about work done for the love of it, not for anybody. Imagine how much at times gets accomplished even while walking in the street, not for anyone's sake, work for the sake of work, work itself being one's only God. This also is one of the states. But if one goes on performing action of this kind, there comes a day when one is liberated from action. There is such a thing as labouring for the welfare of the world, but here even this purpose is absent. It is a type of work not actuated by desire or craving; one just cannot help doing it. Well then, why is it done? One simply is in love with the work. When God manifests Himself in the form of some work, which therefore exercises intense attraction on a particular person, then, by engaging in this work again and again, one is finally liberated from all action

QUESTION: Work only begets more work; how can it come to an end?

MATAJI: Do you not know this? If you can become so completely concentrated in any one direction that you cannot help acting along that line, wrong action becomes impossible. In consequence, action is losing its hold on you and is bound to come to an end. How many states and

[125] Summarized from M. Hiriyanna, *The Essentials of Indian Philosophy*, pp. 51–6.

[126] *Words of Anandamayee Ma*, Varanasi: S.S. Anandamayee Sangha, 1971, pp. 80–3.

stages there are! This is one of them. Here one has certainly not yet attained to Knowledge of the Self, but one cannot act wrongly. Neither is there an opportunity for considering whether one should act in accordance with the *Śāstras* or against them. Nevertheless, in such a state of one-pointedness, wrong action that violates the laws set forth in the *Śāstras* cannot occur. The human body—the vehicle through which the work is being done—has entered a current of purity, and as a result *satkarma,* action in harmony with the Divine Will, is performed.

It is only on the level of the individual that pleasure and pain exists. During spells of severe pain, when one tosses about in burning agony, is there, in spite of attachment to wife, husband, son or daughter, room left for the thought of these loved ones? Does one not groan in a frenzy of self-pity? At that moment the delusion of family ties loses its hold, while the delusion of identifying oneself with the body reigns supreme. One exists oneself, that is why everything exists. From here, on this basis arises the alleged coming and going of the individual, its round of births and deaths.

Now you should understand that one who loves God is but out to destroy identification with the body. When this has come about, there is destruction (*nāśa*)[127] of delusion, of bondage, in other words, of desire (*vāsanā*), of 'not-Self' (*na Sva*). Your dwelling place (*vāsa*) at present is where the Self manifests as 'not-Self' (*na Sva*);[128] when that is destroyed, it is only destruction that is destroyed. Furthermore, what is known as worldly craving, may also be characterized as the activity that takes place because the action of Self-revelation is absent. He is not there, this is the crux of the matter, is it not?

This body tells of yet another aspect—can you guess what it is? Just as the Beloved (*Iṣṭa*) is the Self (*Svaya*), so destruction is also He Himself, and likewise is that which is destroyed. This is so where the Self is and nothing but the Self. Hence with whom can one associate? Therefore it is said that He is without another, existing alone. When speaking of Him as appearing in disguise, what is the disguise? He himself, of course.[129]

[127] 'Here Mataji Ānandamayī Mā plays upon words. *Sva* and *śa* are pronounced alike in Bengali; thus *nāśa* destruction, sounds like *na Sva* "not-Self,"' *Words of Anandamayi Ma,* p. 83 first footnote.

[128] 'Vāsanā, desire, is where the Self dwells as not-Self; *vāsa* to dwell, *na* no, not,' *ibid.*, second footnote.

[129] *Ibid.*, pp. 80–3.

XIX

Varṇa

I

Varṇa, when made to stand for the caste system, poses one of the great challenges to modern Hinduism. The latter has made great advances with regard to the caste system in some respects, while it has been less successful in others. It will help to distinguish between two aspects of the caste system: (1) caste disability, and (2) caste mentality.

Considerable progress has been made, and the corner perhaps been turned, in the matter of removal of caste disabilities. The most striking illustration of this is found in the access that women and the lower castes have gained to the Vedic scriptures, from whose study they were debarred for centuries. This is one aspect of modern Hinduism with respect to which it differs sharply from classical and medieval Hinduism. Professor K. Satchidananda Murty has drawn attention simultaneously to the unfair nature of the restriction, and to its unhappy consequences:

> One of the great obstacles to the preservation and propagation of the Veda has been denial of universal access to it. For several centuries only the traivarṇika men (men of the three upper castes) have been generally considered eligible to undertake Vedic study, but in effect it has been the exclusive privilege and prerogative of male Brāhmins only. Even

today most Brāhmins who have learnt the Veda, either with or without meaning, generally do not teach it to women, śūdras and others.[130]

He goes on to point out that:

...the Veda itself does not say that it is meant for any particular sex, caste or race. On the contrary, it declares that it is meant for all. There is the following Yajurvedic text: 'Just as I have revealed this auspicious word to all human beings, so must you. I have revealed the Vedic truth to Brāhmins, Kṣhatriyas, Śūdras, Āryas, personal servants (*svāya*) and to the lowest of Śūdras (araṇāya) also.' There is also the following Atharvavedic text: 'O Man, I, being of the nature of truth and being unfathomable, have revealed the true Vedic knowledge; so I am he who gave birth to the Veda. I cannot be partial either to a Dāsa (slave) or an Ārya; I save all those who behave like myself (i.e., impartially) and follow my truthful commands.' The Veda is a universal scripture.[131]

The Madras High Court, in another context, has similarly held that the *Gāyatrī Mantra* does not belong to just the Hindus of the higher castes, or even just to Hindus, but to all of humanity. 'It will be anachronistic for any one to contend that the *mantra* signifies or relates to any particular religion,' the judge observed. He also noted that 'the Vedas have always been considered to belong to all mankind and are not limited to any particular religion, race, caste or community.'[132]

The issue of caste, of course, goes for beyond this. It is notable that, despite protest movements from both within and without, what we now identify as the caste system has somehow survived and, in the opinion of some scholars, predictions of its demise are premature. David R. Kinsley for instance, writes:

In India today there is considerable legislation that seeks to ease traditional caste division, and in an increasingly industrialized society, particularly in cities where intercaste contact is necessary, many traditional taboos are being breached or modified. Nevertheless, the caste system is such an integral part of the Hindu tradition and world view that it is unlikely to be fundamentally altered until Hinduism itself is

[130] Murty, K. Satchidananda, *Vedic Hermeneutics*, Delhi: Motilal Banarsidass, 1993, pp. 14–17.

[131] *Ibid.*

[132] The *Times of India*, 31 August 1992, p. 4.

fundamentally altered or disappears. The caste system is not an entity unto itself but part and parcel of the Hindu vision of reality, and as such it is not surprising that it persists strongly to this day and has resisted all but the most minor and gradual changes.[133]

One must distinguish here, in somewhat Weberian fashion, among different understandings of the caste system. Of particular significance is the connection between karma and caste, and the conceptual level at which the connection is forged. For instance, it is possible to blame a person's birth in a low caste on past karma. It is, however, also possible to blame the misery shared by people of all varṇas on their collective karma. To take the argument a step further: Was the racial discrimination practised against the Indians by the British the karmic comeuppance of the caste discrimination practised by the Hindus themselves? When Mahatma Gandhi proposed in this spirit that the enslavement of India was the price it had to pay for the sin of practising untouchability, he was only extending the connection between the caste system and karma beyond its classical pale to account for the experience of all Hindus.

Professor R.N. Dandekar points out that there are 'three main attitudes'[134] towards caste today: (1) that the caste system is divinely or naturally ordained, and must not be tampered with and adhered to as is; (2) that it has become perverted and needs to be reformed, so that some would 'like to see the three thousand or more castes grouped together into the four basic social orders of brāhmans, kshatriyas, vaiśyas, and śūdras and to preserve the caste system in that form'; and (3) that the caste system should be done away with. Dandekar elaborates:

The third attitude toward caste today is that of the social reformers who advocate a complete extermination of castes by all possible means. It is now realized that in spite of geographical, climatic, racial, religious, and linguistic diversity, India possesses a fundamental cultural unity. It is rightly pointed out that the gravest evil of the caste system

[133] Kinsley, David R., *Hinduism, A Cultural Perspective*, p. 175.

[134] Dandekar, R.N., 'The Role of Man in Hinduism', *op. cit.*, p. 149.

is that it has rendered Indian society undemocratic and a sociological myth. One, therefore, feels inclined strongly to support the plea that an active nationwide campaign be launched against caste, both through governmental and private agencies.[135]

Others have expressed themselves more forcefully. Swami Vivekananda, not known for mincing words, declared forthrightly: 'But in spite of all the ravings of the priests, caste is simply a crystallized social institution, which... is now filling the atmosphere of India with stink.'[136] A far more trenchant indictment is made by Govinda Das:

The utter rout, the hopeless breakdown of the whole system of caste is exemplified in every nook and corner of India—from the days of Cyrus, Darius and Alexander, downwards through the bitter agony of the Moslem occupation of the country; the widespread ruins of architecture testifying for all those who have eyes to see or ears to hear that the Hindu polity of those 2500 years has failed to be the bulwark of Hindu faith and the channel for conveying uncontaminated its culture. The Kshatriya has proved a rotten reed in the defence of the country; the Vaishya has not brought wealth to the land, nor the Brahman, learning—unless the useless knowledge of the sacrificial art can be called 'learning.' Judged by the present-day condition of India, it must be said that the caste-system as now working has to be abolished altogether, if the Indian people are to have a new lease of life.[137]

The reference to the prolonged period of foreign servitude in this passage is significant as, according to the logic of the varṇa system, it implies the reduction of all Hindus to a single varṇa, that of śūdra (or, to go back to Ṛgvedic usage, *dāsa*) as Mahatma Gandhi clearly saw.[138]

The Indian government has now adopted a policy of trying to remove caste by means of caste—through reservations based on it, perhaps relying on the proverbial wisdom of removing one thorn with another. In accordance with this, a policy of affirmative action and positive discrimination has

[135] *Ibid.*, p. 150.

[136] Cited in Troy Wilson Organ, *The Hindu Quest for the Perfection of Man*, p. 225.

[137] Cited, *ibid.*, p. 225.

[138] M.K. Gandhi, *Hindu Dharma*, pp. 339, 343.

been introduced on an extensive scale. The hope is that it will undo the caste system by undoing its iniquities. The danger, however, is that it may strengthen rather than weaken caste identities, and arrest the process of disappearance of caste mentality with the disappearance of caste disability.

II

We embark now on a discussion of the famous, or notorious, caste system in Hinduism in more detail.[139] As we do, some clarifications are in order.

First, it should be clearly recognized that there is no *exact* equivalent in Hindu terms of what has come to be called the caste system in the West. At best, the term 'caste system' reflects two concepts in combination, or some might say even confusion—those of varṇa and jāti. This is, however, a minor point, although certainly more than just a quibble.

The next point is major: Why should special opprobrium be attached to the caste system when social stratification is a universal feature of human societies? The same applies to its castigation as hierarchical. We must therefore distinguish clearly among three terms: hierarchism, inequalitarianism, and injustice.

Hierarchy is virtually an universal principle of organization. If one is functioning in a university set-up, for instance, then the odds are that this set-up is characterized by hierarchy. After all, even the teacher is 'above' the students, and probably functions 'under' a head of department. A hierarchy only implies inequality when it becomes frozen in place in some way, based on what might be considered an 'extraneous' consideration—such as birth or age. Similarly, inequality by itself does not imply injustice. If there are two workers, one of whom works twice as long as the other, the wages they receive will be unequal: But is the difference thereby unjust?

[139] See Nicholas B. Dirks; *Castes of Mind: Colonialism and the Making of Modern India,* Princeton and Oxford: Princeton University Press, 2001.

So, what made the caste system so odious? What made it so was that, when encountered around 1800 in India, it offered a *religious justification* for the social stratification that was characterized by a discrimination based on caste, and by the further fact that this caste was based on birth. This religious legitimation was provided by the doctrinc of karma *and* rebirth. It is important to note the link, for arguably even Western religions accept the idea of karma in a nutshell, in the doctrine of a Last Judgement. Once birth in a particular caste and, to a certain extent gender, was related to the quality of one's actions in one's past life, the best way to secure advancement to a higher caste in the next life was to scrupulously discharge one's duties in this one. This is why Max Weber paid the doctrine the left-handed compliment of constituting a 'perfect theodicy'.

It is important to view this system historically as a whole, as it must have appeared to an onlooker at the beginning of the nineteenth century. The overall situation may be depicted as follows:

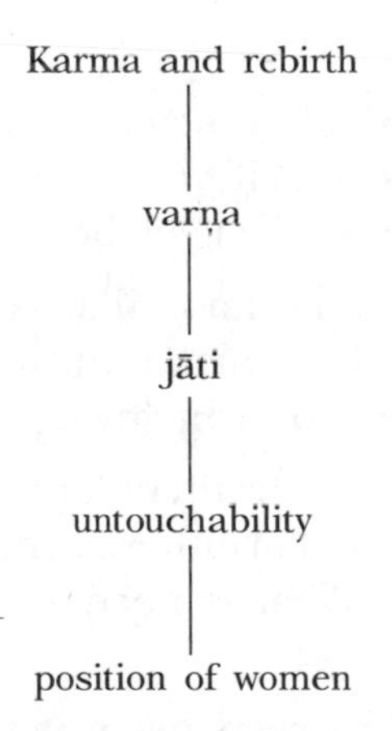

The whole system hung together in a set of interlocking patterns. One's karma in past life determined one's birth (=rebirth) in this life in a particular varṇa—brāhmaṇa, kṣatriya, vaiśya, or śūdra—the order of enumeration involving not just a hierarchy but also a fixed hierarchy.

These varṇas themselves, however, were really made up of smaller units called jātis, constituting typically commensal, endogamous, and craft-exclusive units that, in reality, situated one socially. While the varṇas constitute in principle a functional classification that could be applied to any society, basing them on jāti obscured this aspect, and also made them party to birth-ascription.

Nowhere was this birth ascription clearer and more odious than in the differentiation of the outcastes from the rest of society—on the same principle of birth-ascription. Thus, untouchability was visible proof of the odiousness of the discrimination institutionalized by the caste system.

Gender-differences are also based on birth. Thus, discrimination based on birth also came to dominate gender-differentiation, leading to the low position of women—whose life came to be characterized by such practices as sati, prohibition of widow-remarriage, child-marriage, segregation, etc.

What was the modern response in general to this picture, given the assumption that the whole system was deemed undesirable?

1. The Christian, Muslim, scientific-materialist, and Communist response was that if you want to dissolve the whole system, you must *begin* by giving up belief in karma and rebirth.

2. The Buddhist, Jaina, and Sikh response was that one need not give up belief in karma and rebirth. One can bring the rest of the system down by giving up belief in varṇa.

3. The mainstream modern Hindu response has been that one need not give up belief in either karma and rebirth or varṇa to achieve this result. What is needed is giving up the belief in jāti.

4. Mahatma Gandhi's response was that one need not give up belief in karma and rebirth; and even in varṇa and jāti to achieve the ideal result.

One needs to modify one's understanding of varṇa to realize that such differentiation is present in all societies, and need not involve ideas of 'high' or 'low', as all occupations serve society equally. In this respect, Gandhi's view is consistent with with the mainline modern Hindu view. He departs from it, however, in maintaining that one's means of livelihood must be determined entirely by one's caste. At one stage in his life, Gandhi saw in this a solution to the problem of cut-throat competition of Western societies, which he deplored.

But while Gandhi retained jāti (caste) as a marker for profession, he dissociated it from untouchability and discrimination against women on the ground that, as the untouchables and women belong to the same jāti or race as all human beings by birth, they could not be discriminated against. Here, again, Gandhian thought is in line with mainstream modern Hinduism.

5. Thus, for Gandhi, one did not have to give up belief in karma and rebirth, or varṇa or jāti, but one had to give up belief in untouchability. In this he was opposed by Dr B.R. Ambedkar, who argued that one could not give up belief in untouchability without giving up belief in both varṇa and jāti. However, even Ambedkar did *not* think it necessary to give up belief in karma and rebirth to achieve this result and, when he became a Buddhist towards the end of his life, he retained his belief in karma and rebirth. In doing so, however, he carefully distinguished his Buddhist understanding of rebirth from that of the Hindu. Rebirth in Hinduism involves the reincarnation of the soul, but Buddhism dispenses with the concept of an ātmān, or a soul, transmigrating from one body to another. However, Buddhism accepts the fact of rebirth, while denying reincarnation, by arguing that the previous body, in the process of passing out of being, gives rise to the new one so that no transfer of soul is involved. Ambedkar accepted this concept of rebirth and restricted the concept of karma to action performed now in this life, rejecting its link with karma in past life.[140]

[140] See Babasaheb Ambedkar, *Writings and Speeches*, Vol. 11, Bombay: Education Department, Government of Maharashtra, 1992, pp. 329–44. Also see Gail Omvedt, *Buddhism in India: Challenging Brahmanism and Caste*, New Delhi: Sage Publications, 2003, pp. 269–71.

The following salient features in modern Hindu thought in relation to the caste system are worth nothing.

1. The Hindu category of 'caste' and its relation to the Marxist category of 'class' has been the subject of much discussion in some intellectual circles. It has even given rise to a neologism—'claste'—in the hope that it might combine the explanatory power of both.

2. An interesting feature of the caste system, whose hierarchical structure is usually explained in terms of ritual purity, is its disjunction between wealth and power. Thus, though the practising priest is supposed to be a 'poor brahmin', the 'rich merchant' appears third in the list.

3. Although varṇa and jāti are allied concepts, it is notable that it is the doctrine of varṇa rather than jāti that is the distinguishing feature of Hinduism. One could even say that jāti is an Indian phenomenon, which is also found among Indian Christians and Muslims, as well as Buddhists, Sikhs, and Jains. The concept of the *four* varṇas is more typically Hindu in nature.

4. Modern Hindu thought tends toward the view that caste-discrimination, of which untouchability was the most obvious manifestation, involved serious historical injustice for which the victims need to be compensated. Thus, policies of affirmative action for the former untouchables and other backward classes are firmly in place. Even those who criticize these policies acknowledge that historical wrongs are involved—the difference pertains to the best way of righting them.

The caste system has proven to be of interest in the context of the comparative study of civilization. Edward Digby Baltzell, the likely inventor of the acronym WASP (White Anglo-Saxon Protestant), was a student of the caste system. The acronym WASP, which caught on because 'until then, there was no recognizable way of describing America's ethnic ruling elite', seems modelled on the concept of *dvija*—the male members of the three upper varṇas of Hindu society who constitute a similar elite. Moreover, striking parallels between concepts of caste and nationality—both of which are based on birth but function in a social and a political matrix respectively—have been noticed. Thus, even as one leaves behind the traditional concept of caste, one is struck by its explanatory power in a contemporary context.

III

No account of the caste system in modern Hinduism can be complete without referring to its critique offered by Jyotiba Phule (1827–90),[141] E.V. Ramasami Naicker (1879–1973),[142] and Dr B.R. Ambedkar (1891–1956).[143] The remarkable feature about this trio is that they cover the entire gamut of the caste system. Naicker was a Tamil vaiśya, and hence belonged to the dvija or twice-born class, although he attacked Brahminism; Phule belonged to the lower caste of a gardener, and Ambedkar was born in an untouchable family. All of them were particularly critical of the privileges of the Brahmins, although they differed in their attitude toward Hinduism in general. Naicker condemned not only Brahminism and Hinduism, but also religion per se, in the name of rationalism.[144] Phule attacked the privileges of priesthood, but did not place himself outside the pale of Hinduism.[145] Ambedkar denounced

[141] O'Hanlon, Rosalind, *Caste, Conflict, and Ideology: Mahatma Jyotirao Phule and Low Caste Protest in Nineteenth Century Western India*, Cambridge: Cambridge University Press, 1985.

[142] Diehl, Anita, *Periyar E.V. Ramaswami: The Study of the Influence of a Personality in Contemporary South India*, Bombay: B.I. Publications, 1978; M.D. Gopalkrishnan, *Periyar: Father of the Tamil Race*, Madras: Emerald, 1991.

[143] Omvedt, Gail, *Buddhism in India: Challenging Brahamanism and Caste*, New Delhi: Sage Publications, 2003.

[144] 'For the disappearance of priests and rituals in the Hindu marriages [among his followers], he is chiefly to be held responsible' (D.G.S., *Periyar: E.V. Ramaswamy: A Proper Perspective*, Madras: Vairam Pathippagam, 1975, p. 6).

[145] O'Hanlon, Rosalind, *op. cit.*, p. 239.

Brahminism and renounced Hinduism, but did not go beyond the pale of religion—he embraced Buddhism.[146]

There are other interesting differences among them. Naicker accepted the Aryan invasion theory, and used it to explain how Brahmins came to acquire their privileges and how the Dravidians were driven against the wall.[147] Phule also accepted the Aryan invasion theory and used it to explain how the Brahmins acquired their privileges—but does not seem to play the Dravidian card.[148] Ambedkar, on the other hand, rejected the Aryan invasion theory[149] and explained Brahmin ascendancy in terms of their success in suppressing Buddhism.

They also differed among themselves on the linguistic implications of the Aryan invasion theory. Naicker opposed Sanskrit and Hindi, Phule did not do away with the ritual use of Sanskrit while he did do away with Brahmin priests, and Ambedkar seconded the motion that Sanskrit, rather than Hindi, be accepted as India's official language.[150] We have no record if his views on Sanskrit changed after his conversion to Buddhism.

The critique by these leaders of popular movements leads one to assess the prevalence of principles of social justice within Hinduism.

IV

One must begin by raising the obvious question: What is justice? Although the question is obvious, the answer is anything but so. It cannot be dealt with at length here because, given its inherent intractability, it might take us too far afield. But now that the question has been posed, at least some

[146] Omvedt, Gail, *op. cit.*, p. 261.

[147] D.G.S., *op. cit.*, p. 33.

[148] 'He rather speaks of Shūdras'; see Arvind Sharma (ed.), *Modern Hindu Thought: The Essential Texts*, p. 139 ff.

[149] Ambedkar, B.R., *Who Were the Shudras?*, Bombay: Thackers, 1970 [1946], p. 104.

[150] See The *Hindu*, 11 September 1949. Also see Sumathi Ramaswamy, 'Sanskrit for the Nation', *Modern Asian Studies* 33:2 (1999), p. 353.

response is required to set the discussion in motion. Will Durant answers the question in Platonic terms: 'So Plato replies to Thrasymachus and Callicles, and to all Nietzscheans forever: Justice is not mere strength, but harmonious strength—desires and men falling into that order which constitutes intelligence and organization; Justice is not the right of the strong but the *effective harmony of the whole.*'[151]

We usually quote other scholars to achieve our own ends and this case is no exception, for Plato's definition of justice enables us to identify a crucial component of social justice. This component becomes clear if, at this point, we also introduce two concepts of justice, following Aristotle—distributive justice and rectificatory justice. Distributive justice relates to distribution of rewards, honours, etc. by the state to its citizens. Rectificatory justice, by contrast, 'is the kind of justice which the state seeks to maintain not so much between itself and its members, as between one member and another' of a polity or society.[152] Social justice differs from both these forms of justice, inasmuch that it relates not to the relationship obtained between the state and citizens of a state or among the members themselves, but among the various constituent *groups* within a society (with the state also figuring as one such group). This clarifies, at least to some extent, the meaning of the term social justice, whose presence or absence in Hinduism constitutes the topic under discussion.

The rest of the presentation in this section focuses on Hindu concepts of social justice. One might begin by offering the observation that one knows of no social order under any dispensation—religious or secular—which *claims* to be unjust. That is to say, no religion admits supporting an unjust social order. We may have our own doubts about whether social justice is obtained within such a religious system or not. Even

[151] Durant, Will, *The Story of Philosophy*, New York: Garden City Publishing Co. 1926, p. 48, emphasis added.

[152] Jain, H.M., 'Casteism and the Struggle for Social Justice' (Unpublished paper), Allahabad: Govind Ballabh Pant Social Science Institute, 1995, p. 8.

the self-critical followers of a religion may occasionally—sometimes often—express such doubts, and a religion may even be self-conscious about the absence of social justice within it in certain spheres. But no religion *consciously* sets out to set up a political or social order that in, of, and by itself will be unjust, irrespective of what the ultimate outcome may be. Hindu life and thought must therefore, by assumption, possess a concept or concepts of social organization that it *itself* considers founded on just principles; not just on some principles, but on just principles. Our task then is to prise them out and lift them up to full view. Before these can be unearthed, the ground will have to be cleared with some certain preliminary observations.

The first relates to what may be termed Hindu encyclopedism. Hindu texts tend to be of two types: those that address certain specific areas of knowledge such as medicine, art, etc., and those that may take all knowledge for their province, such as the Vedas, Purāṇas, etc. Even those texts that address specific issues work on the principle of 'acting locally but thinking globally', in a pedagogical rather than geographical sense. As so many topics are thus discussed at many varied places, scholars sometimes hastily, if ironically, conclude that certain topics have not been discussed at all! The situation is sometimes further complicated by the fact that the issues are at times discussed mythically or metaphorically, rather than logically and directly in a cut-and-dried manner.

A second complication is created by the mind-set of the investigator, who approaches the resources of Hinduism with a set notion of the content of the subject. Thus, a scholar may conclude that Hinduism has no ethics because it does not provide anything that conforms to the investigator's own notion of ethics. These considerations prompt one into making the following remarks: (1) In one's search for theories of social justice in Hinduism, one may need to look at texts that *explicitly* address the issues, such as the *dharma śāstras,* as well as those that discuss such issues *implicitly.* Both explicit *and* implicit resources will have to be identified and exploited; (2) Although one may commence such a search with one's own notions of what social justice means or implies, one should leave one's mind open to the possibility that the very concept could be affected, influenced, or even modified by the very search. Any other attitude runs the danger of being limiting, even procrustean.

The second preliminary observation relates to what might be called Hindu pluralism. That Hinduism encompasses within itself a wide variety of viewpoints and styles of life is well known. This means that we might well encounter more than one, or perhaps innumerable, perspectives on issues of social justice. Therefore, rather than describing this section as an exploration of Hindu principles of social justice, what we may actually encounter could perhaps more appropriately be called an outline of views or concepts or ideas or ideals or, better still, perspectives.

This implication of Hindu pluralism—that Hinduism might contain a variety of viewpoints—is fairly obvious. Hindu plurality, however, contains another implication for this section that is both less obvious and more serious in its implications. It has, in fact, a crucial bearing in the present context.

Given the plurality of Hinduism, both at the level of theory and practice, one must now seriously entertain the possibility that the primary concern of Hinduism may be *order* rather than *justice*—its primary thrust is to secure order in the midst of anarchic pluralism that leaves it forever teetering on the brink of greatness and disaster, rather than to secure justice within an already established order. It may be simply too busy establishing order to do so. The manner then, in which it seeks to establish this order, would be the caste system.[153] The ever-present prospect of *varṇa-saṅkara* that weighed so heavily on the minds of the law-givers could well be a palpable, if somewhat metaphorically archaic, expression of this fear of loss of order so precariously and delicately maintained, a fear that is also voiced by Arjuna in the first chapter of the Bhagavadgītā (I.38–46).

[153] Zysk, Kenneth G. (ed.), *The Origins and Development of Classical Hinduism (by) A.L. Basham*, Boston: Beacon Press, 1989, pp. 25–7.

In order to grasp this point fully, one must distinguish between order (*vyavasthā*) and justice (*nyāya*), and clearly grasp the nature of the relationship between the two. Three propositions are crucial to such an understanding: (1) That there can be order without justice, but (2) that there can be no justice without order; in other words, the relationship is not symmetrical—justice presupposes order. And, finally, (3) that an attempt to secure justice—that is, to reorder existing arrangements—disturbs the existing order.

With the help of these conceptual tools, it is now possible to take a fresh look at the caste system in terms of social justice. When the need to maintain order becomes paramount, it becomes rigid, as during the Śuṅga period. When order has been secured, it becomes flexible, that is, more receptive to considerations of justice, as under the Guptas. One need only compare the condition of the Śūdras under the Śuṅgas and the Guptas to assess the force of this point.[154] Finally, once order has been secured and the system thus also feels secure, claims pertaining to the *just* ranking of castes are freely entertained. The concept of order, then, *also* involves the concept of a just order in its broadest understanding. This is illustrated by the story of Aṇīmāṇḍavya.

THE STORY OF AṆĪMĀṆḌAVYA

The story appears in the first *Parvan* (*Ādiparva*) of the Mahābhārata, and its gist as given in the critical edition of the text (as prepared at the Bhandarkar Oriental Research Institute) runs as follows:

> A very renowned ancient seer, known as Aṇīmāṇḍavya, was impaled on a stake, though no thief, on suspicion of thievery. He summoned Dharma, this great seer of yore, and he said, 'When I was a child, I speared a little bird on a stalk of reed. That sin I do remember, Dharma, but none other. Why have my thousand austerities not overcome it? The killing of a Brahmin is worse than the murder of any other creature. Therefore, because of your sin, you shall be born in the womb of a serf!' By this

[154] See Ram Sharan Sharma, *Śūdras in Ancient India*, Delhi: Motilal Banarsidass, 1958, pp. 281–2.

curse Dharma himself was born in the womb of a serf, as a wise, law-observing, sinless body in the form of Vidura.[155]

In order to see the full significance of the story, it is best to turn to the full version of the story in the Mahābhārata and review the story in toto. It is recounted below. The reader may wish to recall the context: It is provided by the birth of Vidura, an incarnation of Dharma himself, as a Śūdra, in the family of the Kurus.

Janamejaya said, 'What did the god of justice do for which he was cursed? And who was the Brahmana ascetic from whose curse the god had to be born in the Sudra caste?

Vaisampayana said, 'There was a Brahmana known by the name of Mandavya. He was conversant with all duties and was devoted to religion, truth and asceticism. The great ascetic used to sit at the entrance of his hermitage at the foot of a tree, with his arms upraised in the observance of the vow of silence. And as he sat there for years together, one day there came into his asylum a number of robbers laden with spoil. And, O bull in Bharata's race, those robbers were being pursued by a superior body as guardians of peace. The thieves, on entering that asylum, hid their booty there, and in fear concealed themselves when the constables in pursuit came to the spot. The latter, observing the Rishi sitting under the tree, questioned him, O king, saying, "O best of Brahmanas, which way have the thieves taken? Point it out to us so that we may follow it without loss of time." Thus questioned by the guardians of peace the ascetic, O king, said not a word, good or otherwise, in reply. The officers of the king, however, on searching that asylum soon discovered the thieves concealed thereabout together with the plunder. Upon this, their suspicion fell upon the Muni, and accordingly they seized him with the thieves and brought him before the king. The king sentenced him to be executed along with his supposed associates. And the officers, acting in ignorance, carried out the sentence by impaling the celebrated Rishi. And having impaled him, they went to the king with the booty they had recovered. But the virtuous Rishi, though impaled and kept without food remained in that state for a long time without dying. And the Rishi by his ascetic power not only preserved his life but summoned other Rishis to the scene. And they came there in the night in the form of birds, and beholding him engaged in ascetic meditation though fixed on that stake became plunged into

[155] van Buitenen, J.A.B. (tr.), *The Mahābhārata*, Vol. I, Chicago and London: The University of Chicago Press, 1973, p. 134.

grief. And telling that best of Brahmanas who they were, they asked him saying, "O Brahmana, we desire to know what hath been thy sin for which thou has thus been made to suffer the tortures of impalement!"'

Vaisampayana said, 'Thus asked, the tiger among Munis then answered those Rishis of ascetic wealth, "Whom shall I blame for this? In fact none else (than my own self) hath offended against me!" After this, O monarch, the officers of justice, seeing him alive, informed the king of it. The latter hearing what they said, consulted with his advisers, and came to the place and began to pacify the *Rishi* fixed on the stake. And the king said, "O thou best of *Rishis*, I have offended against thee in ignorance. I beseech thee to pardon me for the same. It behoveth thee not to be angry with me." Thus addressed by the king, the Muni was pacified. And beholding him free from wrath, the king took him up with the stake and endeavoured to extract it from his body. But not succeeding therein, he cut it off at the point just outside the body. The Muni, with a portion of the stake within his body, walked about, and in that state practiced the austerest of penances and conquered numberless regions unattainable by others. And for the circumstances of a part of the stake being within his body, he came to be known in the three worlds by the name of *Ani-Mandavya* (Mandavya with the stake within). And one day that Brahmana acquainted with the highest truth of religion went unto the abode of the god of justice. And beholding the god there seated on the throne, the Rishi reproached him and said, "What, pray, is that sinful act committed by me unconsciously, for which I am bearing this punishment? O, tell me soon, and behold the power of my asceticism."'

'The god of justice, thus questioned, replied, "O thou of ascetic wealth, a little insect was once pierced by thee on a blade of grass. Thou bearest now the consequences of the act. O Rishi, as a gift, however small, multiplieth in respect of its religious merits, so a sinful act multiplieth in respect of the woe it bringeth in its train." On hearing this, Ani-Mandavya asked, "O tell me truly when this act was committed by me." Told in reply by the god of justice that he had committed it when a child, the Rishi said, "That shall not be a sin which may be done by a child up to the twelfth year of his age from birth. The scriptures shall not recognize it as sinful. The punishment thou has inflicted on me for such a venial offence hath been disproportionate in severity. The killing of a Brahmana involves a sin that is heavier than the killing of any other living being. Thou shalt, therefore, O god of justice, have to be born among men even in the Sudra order. And from this day I establish this limit in respect of the consequence of acts that an act shall not be sinful when committed by one below the age of fourteen. But when committed by one above that age it shall be regarded as a sin."'

Vaisampayana continued, 'Cursed for this fault by that illustrious Rishi, the god of justice had his birth as Vidura in the Sudra order. And

Vidura was well-versed in the doctrines of morality and also politics and worldly profit. And he was entirely free from covetousness and wrath. Possessed of a great foresight and undisturbed tranquility of mind, Vidura was ever devoted to the welfare of the Kurus.'[156]

Nīlakaṇṭha, the sixteenth-century commentator on the Mahābhārata, offers his own comments on the account, which are helpful in the present context. He points out that the rule laid down by Aṇīmāṇḍavya—that a child shall not be held guilty of transgression unless he or she is past a certain age—is in keeping with the position of the Purāṇas. Then he proceeds to add:

The real point involved is the dawn of moral consciousness. And because it is felt that this does not occur until one turns fifteen, that the new limit has been prescribed. The real point involved consists of coming of 'moral age' and not reaching a particular biological age.[157]

In other words, karmic retribution cannot be merely mechanical, it must be moral. To stop with this, however, would be to stop short and miss the significance of the story from the point of view of social justice, which is twofold.

First, it should be noted that children have been treated here as a class, or a group. In other words, the rights of a group within a group are being defined in relation to the collectivity of which it is a part. The ruling of the sage therefore constitutes an example of social justice. It is the second point of significance, however, which is radical to the point of being unnerving. It should not be forgotten that it is Dharma himself, *Justice itself, who is being challenged for being unjust and being punished for it.* In other words, Justice itself is not above justice! This goes beyond nobody being above justice; or even the king not being above justice, or the gods not being above justice; even the god of justice is not above justice.

[156] Ganguli, K.M. (tr.), *The Mahabharata of Krishna-Dwaipayana-Vyasa* (fourth edition), New Delhi: Munshiram Manoharlal Publishers Pvt. Ltd., 1981, pp. 231–3.

[157] For the Sanskrit text see, Laxman Shastri Joshi (ed.), *Dharmakośaḥ* (Wai: Prajñā Pāṭhaśālā Maṇḍala), Vol. I, p. 439.

It should also be noted that it is not just a question here of no one being above the law, but no one being above justice. After all, even law cannot claim to be above justice.

What does all this rhapsodizing about justice amount to? It amounts to the conclusion that in Hinduism, the *concept of social justice is radically empirical.* Obviously, Dharma thought that he was acting justly in punishing Māṇḍavya as he did; but Māṇḍavya did not think so, and punished Dharma.

There is something Rabbinic to the context. It may not be out of place to cite the following account from the Talmud in support of this intuition:

> A number of other famous rabbinical scholars disagreed with Rabbi Elizar's views in regard to a point of ritual law. 'Rabbi Elizar said to them: "If the law is as I think it is then this tree shall let us know." Whereupon the tree jumped from this place a hundred yards (others say four hundred yards). His colleagues said to him, "One does not prove anything from a tree." He said, "If I am right then this brook shall let us know." Whereupon the brook ran upstream. His colleagues said to him, "One does not prove anything from a brook." He continued and said, "If the law is as I think, then the walls of this house will tell." Whereupon the walls of the house began to fall. But Rabbi Joshua shouted at the walls and said, "If scholars argue a point of law, what business have you to fall?" So the walls fell no further out of respect for Rabbi Joshua but out of respect to Rabbi Elizar did not straighten up. And that is the way they still are. Rabbi Elizar took up the argument again and said, "If the law is as I think, they shall tell us from heaven." Whereupon a voice from heaven said, "What have you against Rabbi Elizar, because the law is as he says." Whereupon Rabbi Joshua got up and said, "It is written in the Bible: The law is not in heaven. What does this mean? According to Rabbi *Jirmijahu* it means since the Torah has been given on Mount Sinai we no longer pay attention to voices from heaven because it is written: You make your decision according to the majority opinion." It then happened that Rabbi Nathan [one of the participants in the discussion] met the Prophet Elijah [who had taken a stroll on earth] and he asked the Prophet, "What did God himself say when we had this discussion?" The Prophet answered, "God smiled and said, My children have won, my children have won."'[158]

[158] Fromm, Erich, *Psychoanalysis and Religion*, New haven: Yale University Press, 1950, pp. 45–7. A Hindu parallel to the Rabbinic view is found in the suggestion 'That among the lawgivers also decisions were reached by

In both Hinduism and Judaism, justice, and its concrete manifestation—law ultimately is not something given but something found—through debate, through soul-searching, determined through a wrestling with the angels, or wrested even from the God of Justice itself. It is a struggle—a sublime struggle perhaps, or at times not so sublime—but nevertheless a struggle that you and I cannot afford to shirk. But one is not totally at a loss. The tradition does provide some principles for guidance, some of which are listed below.

The first principle may be identified as a corollary of what is called Natural Law in Hinduism. Its historical roots lie in the concept of dharma as *ṛta*,[159] and its legal roots perhaps in the simultaneous provision for penance and crimes in Hindu law.[160] These themes will be explored elsewhere. At this point, in the context of social justice, the discussion can be moved forward once again with the help of a story.

Once upon a time there was a potter who badly cut his forehead when he fell down on some broken pots. The would healed slowly and left an impressive scar. When a famine occurred, the potter and his family went to another region, where he was seen by a king who admired his size and assumed from his scar that he was a brave fighter. The king put the potter in charge of his army. Shortly thereafter the kingdom was attacked, and as the warriors were about to leave for battle the king happened to ask the potter how he had acquired his scar. When the potter told him, the king was angry and sought to get rid of him. The potter, however, pleaded with the king to be allowed to demonstrate his martial qualities. Thereupon the king told the potter this story:

A lion while hunting once came upon a fox cub, but it was so small that he pitied it and brought it to his wife who had two cubs of her

---

means of deliberation and exchange of opinions. And that at such assemblies the rule of the majority obtained may be argued from certain texts' (Batukanath Bhattacharya, *The Kalivarjyas or Prohibitions in the Kali Age*, University of Calcutta, 1943), p. 172. He cites Kātyāyana (29:12) and Gobhila (III.149) in support.

[159] Griswold, H.D., *The Religion of the Rigveda*, First Indian edition, Delhi: Motilal Banarsidass, 1971; p. 133; etc.

[160] Lipner, Julius, *Hindus: Their Religious Beliefs and Practices*, London and New York: Routledge, 1994, p. 106.

> own. The three cubs were nursed by the lioness and grew up together. One day, while playing together, they saw an elephant pass. The lion cubs, seeing the hereditary enemy, roared and lashed their tails and were going to attack. The fox was afraid, and dissuaded the lion cubs from doing such a foolhardy thing and ran home, followed by the other two cubs. They all told this incident to their mother, who got the fox cub aside and told him who he really was, and said, 'Son, you are brave, and you have learned all there is to learn; you are handsome, but in your line big game is not killed. Go away before my sons realize who you are.'

Having made his point, the king dismissed the potter. Potters are born to make pots. It is their nature, determined by their past actions. To pretend to be something one is not would be disastrous both for the potter and for the safety of the kingdom. It is similar for all castes. Karma and samsara insure that one is born into a situation appropriate to one's predilections, and to try to act like another 'species' is unnatural.[161]

The point is that various varṇas or classes are part of a natural order, and social justice consists in there being a place for everything, and in everything being in its place—just as in the medieval world its division into nobles, the clergy and commoners was considered part of a natural order. Thus, conforming to the caste requirements was just because it was a just—that is, divinely ordained—order.

It is clear that such a theory of natural justice is better described as a theory of social justification rather than one of social justice. Nevertheless, this theory must not be viewed as entirely negative in terms of social justice, for the entire structure, though in itself hierarchical, is capable of being lifted to a higher level, like a production function. It is true that the varṇa concept as mentioned here involves 'the gradation of society into four classes'.[162] But it is equally true that while 'these classes are diversified by their privileges',[163] these

[161] Kinsley, Dabvid R., *Hinduism: A Cultural Perspective*, Englewood Cliffs, New Jersey: Prentice-Hall Inc., 1982, pp. 127–8. The 'Aesop's Fable' in this account is reminiscent of a story in the *Pañcatantra.*

[162] Renou, Louis (ed.), *op. cit.*, p. 52.

[163] *Ibid.*, p. 53.

privileges, when 'negatively interpreted form as many prohibitions',[164] so a sense of justice is not altogether absent.

The second principle may be called the principle of Natural Rights (Dharma as Nyāya). Although the word 'natural' is common to both the first and second principles, its meaning undergoes a sea-change in the two uses. Whereas nature, in the first case, represents Nature with a capital N, and stands for the cosmos, in its second usage it represents human beings in a 'state of nature', vulnerable to destruction. The word nature, in this sense, now acquires a microcosmic dimension, by way of contrast with its earlier macrocosmic understanding. In this state of nature, human beings are visualized as surrendering their rights to the state in return for protection. This is, in a way, a Hindu version of Hobbes' Leviathan. The state is not so monstrous in Locke's version because the human beings here enact two contracts: They enter into contract with each other, and then jointly enter into contract with the state for protection, for safeguarding of their rights to life and property.

Just as a change in the understanding of the word nature—in the semantic shift in its usage from *natural law* to *natural rights*—unlocks the door to a very different concept of social justice in Western thought, the shift in the sense of the word dharma provides the key to unlocking the door to a very different concept of social justice. When the focus of the dharma (as ṛta) is macrocosmic, it tends to coincide with Natural Law; when its focus is microcosmic (dharma as nyāya) it tends to coincide with Natural Rights. As macrocosmic, it is dharma as ṛta, as microcosmic it is dharma as nyāya. This is akin to the doctrine of Natural Law, in which the king was himself part of nature and on equal footing with the subjects, as opposed to the doctrine of Natural Rights in which the king negotiates (himself constituting a component within the whole) the relationship with the common people (another component of the whole), thus bringing the entire arrangement within the purview of social justice. So also in the Hindu case, as

[164] *Ibid.*

described in the Manusmriti (VII,3), people resort to the king to escape anarchy (designated by the expression *mātsyanyāya*)[165] who, like the state in Hobbes and Locke, offers them protection. (The word 'nyāya' in this use has the sense of a maxim as distinguished from its earlier sense of justice.)

The third principle may be called the principle of Human Rights (dharma as satya). The exact relationship of theory of Human Rights to that of Natural Rights is a matter of some debate, but it differs from the latter in that it seeks social justice, not so much in the form of protection *by* the state but as in the form of protection *from* oppression by the state itself. The *locus classicus* of this principle is found in the *Bṛhadāraṇyaka Upaniṣad.* The text is cited below with S. Radhakrishnan's translation and comments:

> 14. *sa naiva vyabhavat. tac chreyo-rūpam atyasṛjata dharmam: tad etat kṣatrasya kṣatraṁ yad dharmaḥ, tasmād dharmād paraṁ nāsti: atho abalīyān balīyāṁsam āśaṁsate dharmeṇa, yathā rājñā evam. yo vai sa dharmaḥ satyaṁ vai tat: tasmāt satyaṁ vadantam āhuḥ, dharmaṁ vadatīti, dharmaṁ vā vadantam, satyaṁ vadatīti: etad hy evaitad ubhayaṁ bhavati.*
>
> 14. Yet he did not flourish. He created further an excellent form, justice. This is the power of the Kṣatriya class, viz. justice. Therefore, there is nothing higher than justice. So a weak man hopes (to defeat) a strong man by means of justice as one does through a king. Verily, that which is justice is truth. Therefore they say of a man who speaks the truth, he speaks justice or of a man who speaks justice that he speaks the truth. Verily, both these are the same.

DHARMA: Law or justice is that which constrains the unruly wills and affections of people.

Even kings are subordinate to dharma, to the rule of law. Law or justice is not arbitrary. It is the embodiment of truth. 'That which is known and that which is practiced are justice.' *jñāyamānam anuṣṭhīyamānaṁ ca tad dharma eva bhavati.* Ś.

Hopes to defeat: *jetum āśaṁsate.* R.

[165] See P.V. Kane, *History of Dharmaśāstra,* Vol. III, (second edition), Poona: Bhandarkar Oriental Research Institute, 1973, pp. 21, 238. Also see A.L. Basham, *op. cit.*, p. 87.

From early times kings are said to act out the truth, *satyam kṛṇvānaḥ.* R.V.X.109.6, or take hold of the truth, *satyaṁ gṛhṇānaḥ.* Atharva Veda V.17.10; satya and dharma, truth and justice are organically related.[166]

Before we turn to Śaṅkara's gloss on the text, it is worth noting how close *satyaṁ gṛhṇānaḥ* of the AtharvaVeda comes to Mahatma Gandhi's term satyāgraha and that when the ṚgVeda text says that the kings practiced truth, it is clear in the light of what has been said above that they practiced justice.

However, the full impact of this passage is felt when it is read with the commentary of Śaṅkara. At the point in the text where it says that in the beginning 'and yet he did not flourish', Śaṅkara raises the question: 'Why did it not flourish?' He then ascribes the failure of *all* the varṇas to flourish to oppression inherent in the machinery of the state (*ugratvāt kṣatrasyāniyatāśaṅkayā*).[167]

The fourth principle that may be identified is what is known as the 'preferential option for the poor' or, more generally, special consideration for the underprivileged. It is significant that this concept applies to women who, as a class or a group, were not to be killed.[168] Thus, significantly, when Hanumān is confronted by the presiding deity of Laṅkā, he does not kill her, but shoves her aside.[169] The *Arthaśāstra* (III.3) provides lighter punishment to women for all crimes, compared to men. This, in its own way, parallels the doctrine of social justice, which advocates preferential option for the underprivileged. The story of Aṇīmāṇḍavya, cited earlier, also addressed the category of children as a class or group.

A dissonant passage from the *Manusmṛti* (III.371) is sometimes cited, for instance by A.L. Basham,[170] that a king should

[166] Radhakrishnan, S. (ed.), *The Principle Upaniṣads*, London: George Allen & Unwin, 1953, p. 170. Ś = Śaṅkara; R = Raṅgarāmānuja.

[167] *Ten Principal Upaniṣads with Śāṅkarabhāṣya*, Delhi: Motilal Banarsidass, 1987, p. 683.

[168] Kane, P.V., *op. cit.*, Vol. II, Part I, pp. 575, 593–4.

[169] Altekar, A.S., *The Position of Women in Hindu Civilization*, Dehli: Motilal Banarsidass, 1962, p. 317.

[170] Basham, A.L., *The Wonder That Was India*, p. 174.

have an adulterous woman literally thrown to the dogs. Two points, however, seem to have been overlooked in this connection. The first is that 'It was only the king who was authorized, to punish a woman to death for adultery with a man of very low caste (vide Gaut. and Manu VIII.371...) *but the king had to undergo a slight penance for doing so* (vide Yāj. II.I.268).'[171] The second point is that even these 'one or two exceptions' ('Gaut. 23.14 and Manu VIII.371') which 'both prescribe that a woman should be devoured by dogs if she has intercourse with a male of a lower varṇa' (vide Vas. Dh. S. 21.1–5) were 'modified later and only *parityāga* was allowed, vide Vas. 21.10, Yāj. I.72'.[172] In fact, 'Viśvarūpa on Yāj. III.264 says that no *prāyaścitta* can expiate for the sin of killing a woman intentionally',[173] as in the case of a *brāhmaṇa*.

Several other provisions of Hindu law in relation to women also seem relevant. Women of all varṇas (except those of the *pratiloma* caste) were tax-exempt.[174] There was special provision for judicial review of cases involving women (Nārada I.43), and they could not be arrested or jailed in certain cases.[175] That women and children were looked upon with legal favour is apparent from the following account:

The general rule that lesser punishment be inflicted on women is stated by Kāt (487) 'In case of all offences, women are to suffer half of the fine in money which is prescribed for a male offender (of the same kind) and when punishment is death for a male, the punishment for a woman would be the excision of a limb.' Kauṭ (III.3) provides: 'a woman attains ability to enter into transactions on completion of 12 years and men when they are 16; if they disobey after that (i.e. after attaining majority) the woman shall be fined twelve paṇas and a man twice that amount.' Aṅgiras quoted by the Mit. (on Yāj. III.243) states that an old man over eighty, a boy below sixteen, women and persons suffering from diseases are to be given half prāyascitta and Śaṅkha quoted by the Mit. (on the same verse) that a child less than five

[171] Kane, P.V., *op. cit.*, Vol. II, Part I, p. 593, emphasis added.
[172] *Ibid.*, p. 575, note 1340.
[173] Kane, P.V., *op. cit.*, Vol. IV, p. 18.
[174] Kane, P.V., *op. cit.*, Vol. II, Part I, p. 595.
[175] Kane, P.V., *op. cit.*, Vol. III, pp. 384–5.

commits no crime nor sin by any act and is not to suffer any punishment nor to undergo a prāyascitta. Under the Indian Penal Code, sec. 82, nothing is an offence which is done by a child under seven years of age.[176]

The fourth principle of social justice embodied in Hinduism is the principle of equality, which is most evident in the operation of caste councils. It is true that the caste system has become a byword for inequality. This impression compromises the fact that equality of treatment prevailed *within a caste* among its members and, in cases brought before the caste councils, decisions were handed out by one's peers. It could be objected that true equality consists in equality of treatment across the board, in relation to all the varṇas. However, it is often not realized that legal discrimination based on varṇa had virtually disappeared by the twelfth century.[177] *Nibandha* literature provides direct evidence on this point. Three such Nibandhas, in which discriminatory provisions on the basis of caste are done away with, may be specifically mentioned: the *Smṛticandrikā* of Devaṇṇa Bhaṭṭa (circa AD 1200); the *Mandanaratna* of Madanasiṁha (circa AD 1425); and the *Sarasvatīvilāsa* of Prataparudra (AD 1496–1539).[178]

The fifth principle of social justice is embodied in the principle of proportionality. Louis Renou noted earlier how elements that appear positively as privileges also appear negatively as prohibitions.[179] Thus, a Brahmin is esteemed on account of his ritual purity, but is forbidden certain kinds of foods. Similarly, some law books lay down higher punishment for the same offence, in keeping with higher-caste status, and it is most remarkable that some law books extend this principle to *all offences*. Thus, in 'the case of theft, Gaut. XII.15–16,

[176] *Ibid.*, pp. 394–5.

[177] Kane, P.V., *op. cit.*, Vol. III, p. 398.

[178] Kane, P.V., *op. cit.*, Vol. II, pp. 378, 375, 377. They are however retained in the *Daṇḍaviveka* (fifteenth century).

[179] Renou, Louis (ed.), *Hinduism*, New York: George Braziller, 1962, p. 53.

Manu VIII.338–9 prescribe that a Vaiśya, a Kṣatriya and a Brāhmaṇa should respectively be fined twice, four times and eight times for the fine imposed on a Śūdra for theft, since each of them is deemed more and more aware of the heinousness of the crime.'[180] Kātyāyana (485) and Vyāsa state this as

[180] Kane, P.V., *op. cit.*, Vol. III, p. 395. Curiously, some scholars interpret the verse as casting the śūdra in a negative light by proposing that 'the habit of stealing is thought to be more usual with him.' This is the author's own reflection, which may or may not have been shared by the law-giver (see R.S. Sharma, *op. cit.*, p. 193). It is clear from Manu's text and the commentaries thereupon, however, that variability is due to the greater sense of responsibility connected with the higher social status ascribed to the upper varṇas (see Manu VIII.337–8, specially 338d). The *Daṇḍaviveka* (a fifteenth-century text), for instance, cites and comments on the verses as follows:

'So Manu (VIII.337–8) says: The punishment for a Śūdra in a case of theft is eight times (the value of the article stolen). It becomes increased sixteen times, thirty-two times and sixty-four times in cases of a Vaiśya, a Kṣatriya and a Brāhmaṇa offender respectively. The punishment may go up to one hundred times or twice sixty-four times (i.e. one hundred and twenty-eight times) in case of the theft having been committed by a Brāhmaṇa, who is (fully or partially) cognizant of the merits and defects of his actions.

D.V. thus comments on the above-quoted verses of Manu: 'Though (Nārāyaṇa) Sarvajña has (in his commentary of Manu) prescribed the above-mentioned three kinds of punishments for a Brāhmaṇa, devoid of merit, a Brāhmaṇa, with some merit and a highly meritorious Brāhmaṇa respectively, yet the merit, spoken of in those cases, is nothing but "knowledge", otherwise the above interpretation (of Sarvajña) comes into conflict with the concluding epithet (of the original text) viz. *tad-doṣa-guṇa-vedinaḥ*, (i.e., those, who are *cognizant of their merits and defects*). Though lenient punishments, being justified, have been accordingly laid down in the cases of Brāhmaṇa and other superior caste offenders in comparison with that, prescribed for a Śūdra criminal, yet commission of an offence by a Brāhmaṇa, etc., who are (fully) cognizant of its condemned character, becomes an occasion for the enhancement of their punishments. Even though such a cognition may sometimes vanish from the mind of an inferior caste person, it does not do so in the case of a member of a superior caste. So the mention of the word *jāti* (i.e., caste) is justified in the discriminatory infliction of punishment. The Ratnākara, which has read the concluding phrase of the above text of Manu as *tad-doṣaguṇa-viduṣaḥ* (thus reading "*viduṣaḥ*" for "*vedinaḥ,*" the former meaning "one who knows, etc.") has

a general rule for all offences.[181] The relevant verses are cited below as the point is rather striking, but seem to have been generally ignored. Kātyāyana states:

yena doṣeṇa śudrasya daṇḍo bhavati dharmataḥ
yena cetkṣatraviprāṇāṁ dviguṇo dviguṇo bhavet

For the same offence for which the śūdra is lawfully punished, the punishment in the case of the kṣatriya and the brāhmaṇa should be progressively doubled.

Vyāsa's statement on the point is even more far-reaching:

prāyaścittaṁ ca daṇḍaṁ ca śaucaṁ cāto yathākramam
kalpyamutkṛṣṭamutkṛṣṭe madhyam madhye' dhame' dhamam.

Repentance, punishment and purificatory rites should be the highest for the highest, medium for the middling and the least for the lowest (class).

The sixth and seventh principles of social justice provide for change in social patterns to secure social order and justice to keep up with changing times or with historical change, and for handling situations of social crisis or breakdown, so that even *in extremis* some semblance of social order and justice could be preserved. Students of Hinduism are familiar with the concept of *varṇāśramadharma,* or dharma which uses one's class or station in life as a point of reference. But 'just as we can speak of dharma only with reference to some class or situation, and for this reason it is always qualified by person and situation, so also there is a relativity in the concept of dharma caused by time and age (*yuga*). The doctrine of *yugadharma,* which introduces an element of

---

made the above sense clearer. We have quoted the above two texts of Manu from the original *Manu-smṛti* which have been rendered more explicit by a text from another authority, which is of Kṣatriya and a Brāhmaṇa should be successively increased by two times than that of a Śūdra in specific offences' (Bhabatosh Bhattacharya (tr.), *Daṇḍaviveka of Vardhamāna Upādhyay,* Calcutta: The Asiatic Society, 1973, pp. 27–8.)

[181] Kane, P.V., *op. cit.,* Vol. III, p. 395.

adaptation and adjustment, has a parallel in the concept of *āpaddharma*.'[182]

It might be argued that these principles are merely passive, that they are merely instruments of accommodation to existing realities, not means of changing them. To the extent that such accommodation helps rectify unjust distortions that may emerge in societies over time, they may not be overlooked, but they can hardly be applauded as an engine for securing social justice. The question must be put bluntly: Does Hinduism provide any instrumentality for initiating a social revolution—not just social accommodation, not just social amelioration, but social revolution?

An eighth principle seems to provide for this, although it does not sound very revolutionary to begin with. V. Raghavan has argued that there is a key distinction to be identified in interpreting the *Manusmṛti*—the distinction between a lower dharma and a higher dharma, the former being pravṛtti and the latter nivṛtti. It should be noted that this distinction is drawn here in relation to dharma itself, and not to mokṣa, another context in which this distinction is applied. He writes:

> The apparently divergent statements on taking a Śūdra wife, resorting to *niyoga* (levirate) and eating flesh found in the work are not really contradictory, for they are based on the doctrine of *nivṛttistu mahāphalā* (greater benefit from abstention) which Manu himself enumerates and which is basic to the approach and philosophy of Manu and of Hinduism as moulded by Manu and other teachers.[183]

It is when Raghavan alludes to this distinction later that germs of a doctrine of at least social transformation, if not revolution, become discernible. He picks up the thread as follows:

> As pointed out already, there is a lower dharma in which a thing is permitted, and a higher dharma where refraining from it is considered more meritorious and fruitful. No doubt this dharma is the same satya, but Manu says that for enforcing it, one should not adopt any violent

[182] Raghavan, V., 'The Manu Saṁhitā', in *The Cultural Heritage of India*, Haridas Bhattachartya (ed.), Vol. II, Calcutta: The Ramakrishna Mission Institute of Culture, 1975, p. 342.

[183] Raghavan, V., *op. cit.*, p. 338.

or severe methods; thus the same dharma which is satya is also ahiṁsā (non-violence). This uniqueness is best brought out in the verse:

> *satyam brūyāt priyam brūyāt brūyāt na satyampriyam*
> *priyaṁ ca nānṛtaṁ brūyāt eṣa dharmaḥ sanātanaḥ* [184]

Speak the pleasant truth, never the unpleasant truth. Only speak the pleasant truth—such is the immemorial moral tradition.

This verse has all the right words—satya, *anṛta*, dharma, sanātana—but its purport is too polite to be exciting, to say nothing of being revolutionary. For the revolutionary combination of satya and ahiṁsā one has to turn to Mahatma Gandhi, who mentions some familiarity with the *Manusmṛti* in the formative years of his life.[185]

The ninth principle is provided by conscience. Thus, when Gandhi, while still in his teens, was asked by his parents not to play with his untouchable friend, Uka, although he was devoted to them, he told them that he considered this wrong.

> It was a time when he was beginning to think seriously about morality and codes of conduct. He was twelve, in his second year at the high school, when he began to question the accepted codes of the Indian caste system. A scavenger called Uka, who belonged to the lowest caste, was employed in the house to clean out the latrines. If anyone of a superior caste accidentally touched the scavenger, then he must at once purify himself by performing his ablutions. Mohandas had a great fondness for Uka and could see no reason why he was regarded as inferior. Very respectfully he suggested to his parents that they were wrong to regard the scavenger in this way; an accidental touch could not be a sin and Uka was a man like other men. His mother reminded him that it was not necessary to perform one's ablutions after touching a scavenger; instead, one could touch a Muslim, thus transferring the pollution to someone who was free of the taboos of the Hindu religion.[186]

[184] *Ibid.*, p. 343. The verse cited at the end of the passage may be translated as follows: 'Speak the pleasant truth, never the unpleasant truth. Only speak the pleasant truth: such is the immemorial moral tradition.'

[185] Mahatma Gandhi, however, formed a very different impression from his reading of it. See *Gandhi: An Autobiography*, Boston: Beacon Press, 1993, pp. 34, 325.

[186] Payne, Robert, *The Life and Death of Mahatma Gandhi*, New York: E.P. Dutton, 1969, p. 34.

The slaying of Śambūka by Rāma is well known. The incident is described in the sixty–seventh chapter (according to the critical edition) of the *Uttarakāṇḍa* of the Rāmāyaṇa. The son of a Brahmin dies prematurely even during the ideal reign of king Rāma. Rāma consults the sages for an explanation and is told that it is the tragic result of a *Śūdra* practicing austerities (*tapas*) in his kingdom, the practice of which is forbidden to the *Śūdras* at the time Rāma was ruling. Rāma seeks him out and slays Śambūka, for that was his name, whereupon the dead child comes back to life. While this incident is well known it is not equally well known that an illustrious ancestor of his royal line, Māndhatā, refused to slay a Śūdra under comparable circumstances, according to an account found in the *Padma Purāṇa.*[187] Although it might be argued that only individuals have a conscience, the consequence of acting according to it are surely social, as the prophetic tradition within the Judeo-Christian tradition testifies. This point is often overlooked in the discussion of Hinduism, and needs to be developed further.

The principle of justice in Hinduism, at the level of the individual, acts through the doctrine of karma, and at the level of the collectivity the principle of justice acts through the doctrine of dharma. This involves a slight asymmetry. The principle of karma is the principle of individual *justice,* some loose ends notwithstanding.[188]

This point emerges more clearly when we consider the philosophy underlying each. The individual, the jīva, the bearer of karma is considered *anādi,* or without a beginning in time. Were one to posit a beginning, it will involve an *original* endowment—and that would involve arbitrariness. Hence, no beginning is posited and the complete justice of the doctrine is sought to be secured thereby.

Hindu thought tends to be order-oriented rather than justice-oriented, just as it tends to be duty-oriented rather than rights-oriented, without negating either.

[187] Lefeber, Rosalind (tr.), *Rāmāyaṇa of Vālmīki,* Vol. IV, Princeton, New Jersey: Princeton University Press, 1994, p. 244 note 31.

[188] See Manu VIII.317, etc.

In strict obedience to this order, the sun rises in the east and sets in the west, night and day follow each other and the seasons change. Order is the universal bond that holds the world together; order assigns a place to all created things. Order is universally sought and esteemed. *Those who oppose order are not against it on principle, they only renounce the existing order of things, but not order itself.*[189]

In the case of society, however, a beginning is posited, whether involving harmony or anarchy. From either—as a negative or positive development—kingship, i.e., hierarchy, emerges that is necessary for order. Once order is in place, the painful question arises: Is individual justice to be sacrificed to maintain social order? Is it because the Hindu lawgivers felt so secure in the operation of the doctrine of karma that individual injustice was perceived as inconceivable—leading to a virtually exclusive focus on order?

The gradual amelioration of discrimination and severity of punishment, however, marked the succeeding development progressively in the case of both views—which posited an initial harmony or an initial anarchy. It ended in egalitarianism. If order broke down leading to anarchy, this was characterized by the predominance of Śūdras—an approximation to one varṇa. The *Matsya Purāṇa* carries this point to the logical conclusion: There will be only one varṇa in Kaliyuga, the Śūdra.[190] All became equal.

Whether the initial condition was one of harmony or anarchy, once it had passed through the phase of order, it culminated in either anarchic or paradisical egalitarianism—or one followed by the other, as Kṛta Yuga succeeded Kali Yuga.

It seems, then, that the karmic pattern for the individual is essentially one—but the dharmic is twofold. One line of development is from anarchy→order→justice, as *happens* with the development of the dharmaśāstras. The other has harmony→ order→with declining harmony ending in anarchy and

[189] Panda, K.B., *Sanatana Dharma and Law*, N.P.: 1977, p. 22, emphasis added.

[190] Olivelle, Patrick, *The Āśrama System: The History and Hermeneutics of a Religious Institution*, New York: Oxford University Press, 1993, p. 236, note 53.

then restoration of harmony, the development as it is *supposed to happen* according to the dharmaśāstras, or the standard view.

Individual justice thus suffices by itself as society goes through these gyrations. It is a perfect fit. The difficulty is that, given the doctrine of karma, it will always be a perfect fit. Social, economic, and political justice, by contrast, must be sought on its own—hence the need for an independent arthaśāstra, apart from the dharmaśāstra.

Individual justice is automatic. Social, political, and economic justice is 'manumatic'. Or, to vary the metaphor: Individual justice is ever in neutral, to be shifted into any gear by the driver of the car, depending upon where he or she wants to go and at what speed.

The doctrines of karma and dharma make it clear that justice is a process. It is dharma that accounts for karma at the cosmic level, and it is karma that accounts for dharma at the social level. Both are open-ended.

Justice is grounded in truth in the earliest speculations in Hinduism. This imparts new significance to the title of Mahatma Gandhi's autobiography, *The Story of My Experiments with Truth.* It implies that those stories are also stories of experiments with justice, which will always continue. They have been continuing not only at the individual level, but also at that of society.

In this setting of *Sanatana Dharma* and *Law*—the former embracing the latter in the pre-historic age, they landed on the historic age. *In this age, the centre of gravity shifted from Sruti to Smriti and then to custom.* Custom pre-supposes the juristic sentiment of people, and certain external, constant, and general acts by which it is shown. It takes its birth in some need felt by the society; and satisfaction of such need might have been obtained, in the beginning, through some transitory and isolated acts gradually giving rise to a general conviction of the necessity of such satisfaction. The acts would develop into a customary law of people. Custom thus necessarily involves two conceptions, first the conviction, and secondly the constant and general use; and these two bear to each other the relation of a basic principle and an external expression. *Gautama* in connection with the administration of justice by the king has said; 'The customs of countries, castes and families, which are not opposed to the sacred records have also authority.' Great *Manu*, as we have seen regards approved usage as direct evidence of law. The expression generally used by the *Smritikaras* for custom are *Achara*, *Sadachar* and *Shishtachara*. Broadly said they mean practice of good men which necessarily involves an element of reasonableness, [and] should have no vestige of moral turpitude or anything opposed to public policy.[191]

This axis has shifted to individual conscience in the modern age. Perhaps each source of dharma enunciated by Manu (II.6; 12) could be correlated with each age (I–85)—for the nature of dharma changes with each age (I.85–86). Through this set of correspondences, śruti would be the main source of dharma for the Kṛta age; smṛti for Tretā; ācāra for Dvāpara, and ātmatuṣṭi for Kali!

The tenth principle of social justice is embodied in the concept of *daṇḍa*. Dharma is morally associated with non-violence, but politically it is linked with coercion—and *both* may be considered as valid means for achieving social justice, when the history of Hinduism is taken into account from ancient to recent times. After surveying the relevant references to daṇḍa, for instance, P.V. Kane concludes:

The conception of daṇḍa is therefore this, that the state's will and coercive power keep the individual and nation within the bounds of dharma, punish for breaches, and effect the good of the whole. The gods, *dānavas*, gandharvas, the rākṣasas, and reptiles—these also tend to bring about enjoyment for men because they are pressed down by daṇḍa (Manu Vii.23). The Bhagavadgītā (X.38) identifies daṇḍa with the divine Kṛṣṇa 'I am daṇḍa in the hands of those who control others, I am *nīti* (i.e., rājanīti) for the conquerors.' For the detailed effects and long eulogies of daṇḍa, vide Manu VII.14–31, Matsya 225, 4–17, Kāmandaka II.38–44. These eulogies of daṇḍa presuppose the theory that people obey law and the dictates of the śāstra through the fear of force or punishment. Daṇḍa should be neither too severe nor too mild, but should be appropriate to the fault committed (Kaut. I.4, Kāmandaka II.37, Manu VII.16, Śānti 15.1ff, Śānti 56.21, 103.34).[192]

[191] Panda, K.B., *op. cit.*, p. 91, emphasis added.
[192] Kane, P.V., *op. cit.*, Vol. III, p. 22.

P.V. Kane then proceeds to demonstrate the immediate implications of this principially remote concept for the individual:

Śānti 57.41 advises that one should first secure a king, then wife, then wealth, for in the absence of the ruler there would be no wife nor private property. This shows that the institutions of family and private property and the protection of the weak are bound up with the existence of a ruler. Kātyāyana says the king is the protector of the helpless, the home of the homeless, the son of the sonless, and the father of the fatherless.[193]

The *Mā-Bāp* or paternalistic concept of the Birtish Raj then appears as another imperially recycled incarnation of this concept.

Another dimension of social justice within Hinduism is enshrined in the concept of yugadharma, or the idea that certain usages are appropriate in certain yugas or ages, but not in others. The relevance of this concept to social justice becomes immediately apparent when it is realized that social justice, although referred to as a 'social' justice, has a strong historical component to it, and often involves the righting of historical wrongs. It was earlier mentioned as the sixth principle and may now be discussed in detail.

The principle of yugadharma operates in general and specific ways. The first general way in which it operates is through the provision that 'the dharmas prescribed for men in each yuga differ.'[194] Not only is this stated as such in Manu (I.85) but the different dharmas for the different ages are also specified as follows (I.86):

Kṛta	*Tapas* (austerity)
Tretā	Knowledge
Dvāpara	Sacrifice
Kali	Charity

The second general way in which it operates is by assigning the status of authority to different smṛtis in different yugas.

[193] *Ibid.*, pp. 22–3.
[194] *Ibid.*, p. 892.

According to the *Parāśarasmṛti* (I.24), for instance, this distribution follows the following pattern:

Kṛta	Manusmṛti
Tretā	Gautama[195]
Dvāpara	Saṅkhalikhita
Kali	Parāśara

The importance of this distribution may be gauged from the fact that out of all these smṛtis as we know them, Parāśara alone seems to provide expressly for the remarriage of widows. The fact that it applied to *our* age even caused problems for that period in the history of Hinduism when remarriage of widows came to be frowned upon, so that a different 'reading was fabricated by orthodox people'.[196]

This leads one to the specific way in which the doctrine of yugadharma has been invoked, namely, that certain practices are forbidden in a certain yuga. Such a list of forbidden dharmas is specially drawn up for Kaliyuga. Thus, P.V. Kane, in his monumental *History of Dharmaśāstra,* refers to several practices forbidden in the Kaliyuga.[197] One of his observations is particularly relevant here:

It is remarkable in this connection to note that, though the Parāśarasmṛti (in I.24) claims par excellence to lay down the dharmas for the Kali age, several important provisions contained in it, viz., the remarriage of a married woman (Parāśara IV.30), the variation in the period of impurity due to births and deaths depending on the learning and character of a brāhmaṇa (Parāśara III.5–6), permission to partake of the food of five classes among śūdras (XI.21) *are included among Kalivarjyas* by the Ādityapurāṇa (as quoted by writers of the 12th and later centuries).[198]

[195] T.M.P. Mahadevan cites Parāśara as assigning Yājñavalkya to Tretā, *Outlines of Hinduism,* Bombay: Chetana, 1971, pp. 32–3). I have followed P.V. Kane (*op. cit.*, Vol. III, p. 892).

[196] *Ibid.*, p. 885, note 1730. The reading *patiranyo vidhīyate* was changed to *patiranyo na vidyate*!

[197] Kane, P.V., *op. cit.*, Vol. II, pp. 151, 162, 424, 451, 603, etc.

[198] *Ibid.*, Vol. III, p. 885, emphasis added.

From a modern point of view, which favours the remarriage of widows, the operation of the kalivarjya would seem regressive. It should be carefully noted, however, that although its *application* here is regressive, the *principle* underlying it is essentially progressive. Three distinct but connected observations made by P.V. Kane deserve special consideration in this respect. First, he notes:

Social ideas and practices undergo substantial changes even in the most static societies. Many of the practices, that had the authority of the Veda (which was supposed to be self-existent and eternal) and of such ancient smṛtis as those of Āp., Manu, and Yāj., had either come to be given up or had become obnoxious to popular sentiment. This fiction of great men meeting together and laying down conventions for the Kali age was the method that was hit upon to admit changes in religious practices and ideas of morality.[199]

This naturally prompts the allied observation that if social usages are subject to change, then the alleged immutability of dharma is illusory or, as he puts it:

The Kalivarjya texts are also a complete answer to those who hold fast to the notion that dharma (particularly *ācāradharma*) is immutable and unchangeable (*aparivartanīya*). This chapter on Kalivarjya unmistakably shows how the most authoritative dicta of the Veda and of ancient sages and law-givers were set aside and held to be of no binding authority because they ran counter to prevailing notions and furnishes a powerful weapon in the hands of those who want to introduce reforms in the institutions of marriage, inheritance, and other matters touching modern Hindu society.[200]

Finally, it must also be recognized that forbidding a practice in principle or by 'legislation' as anachronistic may not involve its actual cessation, even when it has been deprived of legitimacy in this manner. Thus, 'One can further see how some practices still persist in spite of the prohibitions in Kalivarjya texts viz. marriage with one's maternal uncle's daughter, sannyāsa, agnihotra, and even sautra animal sacrifice (rarely).'[201]

[199] *Ibid.*, p. 967.
[200] *Ibid.*
[201] *Ibid.*

One particular principle of social justice in Hinduism deserves special consideration, both from a traditional and modern point of view—the principle of compensation. In an ancient story, a kite chases a pigeon, which lands in the lap of king Śibi. The kite demands to be compensated for the loss of its meal, whereupon the king offers his own flesh in return.[202] If the incident is transferred to a human context, it is clear that the loss of subsistence must be compensated for. A similar situation arises in the case of King Dilīpa, and he offers himself to a lion in lieu of a cow.[203] The motif is therefore a pervasive one, and has taken the form of compensating the untouchables for past wrongs in modern times. This context is significant in many ways. Foremost, it allows for the specific formulation of the concept of social justice in the Indian context. H.M. Jain states that in the present-day Indian context, social justice would mean:

(1) Social equality, such as the one enshrined in Article 15 (2) of the Indian Constitution:

> No citizen shall, on grounds only of religion, race, caste, sex, place of birth or any of them, be subject to any disability, liability, restriction or condition with regard to—
>
> (a) Access to shops, public restaurants, hotels, and places of public entertainment; or
>
> (b) The use of wells, bathing *ghats*, roads and places of public resort maintained wholly or partly out of state funds or dedicated to the use of the general public.

(2) Equality of opportunity for all citizens in matters relating to employment or appointment to any office under the state, such as the one guaranteed under Article 16 (1) of the Indian Constitution.

(3) Prohibition of discrimination among citizens on grounds of only religion, race, caste, sex, descent, place of birth, residence, or any of them for purposes of employment under the state.

(4) Freedom to practice any profession or to carry on any occupation, trade, or business, and

[202] Mani, Vettam, *Purāṇic Encyclopedia*, Delhi: Motilal Banarsidass, 1975, pp. 715–16.

[203] *Ibid.*, pp. 241–2.

(5) Freedom to reside and settle in any part of the territory of India.[204]

Such a formulation of the concept of social justice will be considered incomplete, if not inadequate, by many Hindus nowadays. A stronger version would include preferential treatment of the Scheduled Castes, Scheduled Tribes, and other backward classes in the form of (1) reserved seats in legislatures; (2) reserved posts in governments, and (3) special educational and economic aid. The issue is a contentious one, but the concept of social justice within Hinduism has now certainly come to embrace the 'amelioration of the downtrodden and the deprived sections of society'.[205] In traditional terms, it may be viewed as an extension of concept of ṛṇa or 'indebtedness' to and from certain elements within the cosmos to those within society.

In concluding this section, I would like to address the question of social justice at its broadest, both from a general and a Hindu perspective. First, a question: Are we aware of any social, political, or economic system—or any system in general, for that matter (short of utopias)—that we would be willing to pronounce as an absolutely perfect example of social justice in every possible way? I suspect that the answer would be in the negative. Social justice, as noted earlier, has to do with relationships among the constituent parts of a system. Since the current concern with issues of social justice in India is at least related to, if not inspired by, the West, let us look at some of the models that have been developed in the West to produce the desired results.

The totalistic communist model has virtually collapsed. Even in its heyday, it seemed to seriously compromise the rights of the individual. The national democratic model seems to have been more successful but, while it celebrates individual rights of peoples, their solidary rights in terms of health care, etc., it seems, are often compromised. If we now turn to the international sphere and treat the globe as a whole, of which

[204] Jain, H.M., *op. cit.*, pp. 8–9.
[205] *Ibid.*, p. 16.

the nation-states are part, then it is only recently that even the right to development has been fully conceded to them. In other words, despite all the hue and cry about social justice, it is perhaps in some ways as conspicuous by its absence in the West itself, as in the rest of the world. This prompts the salutary realization that, although there might be Hindu or non-Hindu theories of justice, they are just that—theories about a more intractable reality. In fact, given the dynamic nature of the world we live in—indeed, given the dynamic nature of the universe we live in—it might be doubted if complete social justice can ever be achieved at any point in time.

This is, however, not a counsel of despair: the point is intellectual in its import—that perhaps, in order to get rid of social injustice, one will have to get rid of social distinctions, to begin with. The point may be elaborated through a Hindu perspective associated with Vedānta, for explaining which an understanding of certain Sanskrit terms is essential. The first set consists of the terms *abheda* and *bheda*. Abheda, that is to say the absence of bheda, implies the absence of distinctions, as the word bheda stands for distinctions. There are three kinds of such distinctions, according to a popular classification: *vijātīya, sajātīya,* and *svagata.* The distinction called vijātīya applies to objects that belong to different classes, for instance, the difference between cars and trees. They are not only different from one another, but represent two different classes of objects. However, not only can a tree be different from a car, but one tree is also different from another tree, although they both belong to the same class. This kind of difference is termed sajātīya. Further, not only may one tree be different from another, but the various elements that constitute the tree also differ from one another. Thus a leaf is different from a branch, which in turn differs from a trunk. Such differences are called svagata, or internal divisions.

These categories can be applied to that Hindu social phenomenon central to the discussion of social justice in Hinduism, namely, the caste system. It is well known that the caste system combines the two concepts of jāti and varṇa. Jātis are connubially and commensally exclusive groups that are often also craft exclusive. They are numerous, and *birth ascription is crucial to this category*. The varṇas represent a division of society into classes in terms of primary occupational orientations. Whether their membership is based on birth alone, or birth plus worth, or worth alone, has been a subject of constant debate within the tradition. The varṇas are four in number. The jātis are numerous and theoretically related to varṇas, but in practice function more or less independently. The relationship among the jātis *per se* is more important that of the jāti to a particular varṇa. In fact, the jātis represent the extreme elaboration of the caste system, carried to the point of proliferation. The distinctions among them may be regarded as vijātītya, as they could be considered as separate 'species'. The point may be developed further with the help of a famous dialogue between Nahuṣa and Yudhiṣthira in the Mahābhārata. In it, the whole of humanity is depicted as belonging to one jāti or race, that of humanity, and the membership of a varṇa is strictly based on qualities. Thus, inasmuch as human beings belong to one race but differ in aptitudes, these differences of varṇa may be considered sajātīya, when the term jati is used to designate the human race.

It is worth noting that, as one moves from the category of vijātītya bheda to sajātīya bheda, the problem of social justice becomes less acute. Most of the battles for social justice within the vijātītya category were fought on issues of precedence—vis-à-vis another jāti—or pertained to the varṇa to which the jāti was about to be affiliated, etc. At the level of sajātīya bheda, they were greatly reduced, and some issues virtually disappeared.

If, however, one turns to one of the earliest statements on the origin of the varṇas, they are depicted as emerging from the head, arms, thighs, and feet of the cosmic being called *Puruṣa*. They thus denote an organically unified society, and the distinctions between them are internal anatomical divisions in the body of the Puruṣa—in which the varṇas represent svagata-bheda. Their organic unity further drastically reduces chances of dissonance, which might raise issues of social justice, among them.

But distinctions, though internal, still persist. We may now turn to another paradigm that explains the emergence of the four varṇas differently. It is alluded to earlier in the passage cited from the *Bṛhadāraṇyaka Upaniṣad.* According to this model, each later varṇa emerges from the previous one. They are also represented as ideal types in heaven. The earthly varṇas are divinized, as it were, and therefore escape the trammels of social justice by being divinized. However, when distinctions are related to the divine person or in the divine world, presumably the distinctions do not count for much.

Such an approach, however, dissolves rather than solves the question of social justice, which in some religions is resolved by an appeal to radical equality. This is the point at which, in Islam, all human distinctions disappear in the presence of Allah, or the point at which in Christianity slave and master, Jew and Gentile become one in Christ. There are signs however, that the Hindu tradition travels further down this road.

The occasion for developing the theme further is provided by the following incident in the life of Śaṅkara, a renowned Hindu thinker usually assigned to the ninth century:

> When he was staying at Kāsī a startling incident is said to have occurred.... One day while he was proceeding towards the river with his disciples he met a Cāṇḍāla on the way and asked him to move away. The Cāṇḍāla, however, promptly pointed out the contradiction between the Vedantic idea of spiritual unity and the caste notion of untouchability. Śaṅkara was quick to realize his error. Whether the Cāṇḍāla was Śiva himself in human form or whether Śaṅkara realized that the Cāṇḍālas like all beings, could not be anything other than Śiva, are merely the same fact represented mythically or philosophically. The incident could hardly be a fabrication of later times when such repudiation of untouchability or caste-inequality was unthinkable within orthodoxy.[206]

This is a significant narrative from the point of view of the present discussion. However, although its significance

[206] Chandra Pande, Govind, *Life and Thought of Śaṅkarācārya*, Delhi: Motilal Banarsidass, 1994, p. 87.

has been realized by scholars like S. Radhakrishnan[207] and K. Satchidananda Murty,[208] it still remains to be fully explored.

A fresh understanding of the varṇa system in spatial terms seems to be called for, in order to undertake such an exploration. One may commence with the realization that as one moves down the varṇa hierarchy, the conceptual area of concern narrows like a cone. For example, the brāhmaṇa is concerned with the whole world; indeed, the universe constitutes his area of concern. The area of concern of the kṣatriya, while still quite large as it covers the entire kingdom, is still smaller than that of the brāhmaṇa. The area of concern of the vaiśya, consisting not of spiritual but temporal or business concerns is even narrower, while that of the śūdra, concerned as he is with serving those in his immediate environment, is still more narrow. Thus, the conceptual area of concern of each member of the varṇa gradually declines as one moves down the hierarchy. By way of contrast with the conceptual area of concern, however, the geographical area of activity of the various varṇas provides a mirror image of gradual contraction. Thus, the śūdra can move around freely all over the world, (*Manusmṛti* II–24); the vaiśya travels widely on account of his business interests (*Manusmṛti* VIII.157). The kṣatriya is confined to his kingdom, while the preferred area of residence of the brāhmaṇa is even more limited (*Manusmṛti* II–17–23).

The encounter between Śaṅkara and the Cāṇḍāla is thus a remarkable challenge to the limitations of both—the geographical limitation of the brāhmaṇa and the conceptual limitation of the cāṇḍāla. It should be noted, in the context of social encounter as a catalyst of social justice, that each one has overcome their respective limitation. Śaṅkara, although a brāhmaṇa, is a globe-trotter as far as India is concerned,[209] and the Cāṇḍāla is an Advaitin.

[207] Radhakrishnan, S., *The Brahma Sūtra*, London: George Allen and Unwin Ltd., 1960, pp. 162–3.

[208] Murty, K. Satchidananda, *Inauguration Address: Rashtriya Sri Shankaracharya Jayanti Mahotsava*, New Delhi: Vijyan Bhavan, 1988, pp. 8–9.

[209] Pandey, Govind Chandra, *op. cit.*, p. 337.

The significance of the encounter, however, is not as yet exhausted for, as a sannyāsī, Śaṅkara is beyond all ritual pollution, just as the śūdra is said to be free from sin.[210] There is a social injustice involved, not merely in modern but even in traditional terms, on the part of Śaṅkara in asking the untouchable to move away qua untouchable. But the plot thickens. Although, as a śūdra one can move about as one pleases, an *untouchable*'s movements are restricted. Faxian, the Chinese traveller who visited India c. 400 C.E., informs us that they had to announce their arrival in a village, so that the people could avoid pollution.

However, technically, the untouchable falls into the category of the śūdra according to the Manu (X–v), as there is no fifth varṇa. In other words, both Śaṅkara and the Cāṇḍāla find themselves trapped in spheres of circumscribed universality. Śaṅkara is a brāhmaṇa who is now a sannyāsī, and the untouchable is an untouchable who is also a *Śūdra*—yet both have compromised their universality and have drawn invisible lines that do not really exist. Thus, the text called *Śaṅkara Digvijaya* states that Śaṅkara lost sight of the untouchable as it were, and beheld lord Śiva instead. The last line describing the encounter may be translated as follows:

> Filled with fear, devotion, humility,
> faith, joy and wonder,
> the devout Śaṅkara began
> to praise Śiva on beholding
> His eight forms. (6.40)

The Sanskrit text of the first line might intrigue readers, and is now cited: *bhayena bhaktyā vinayena dhṛtyā yuktaḥ sa harṣeṇa ca vismayena.* In the eight forms of Śiva that are referred to, space, sun, moon, etc., figure prominently. In other words, all distinctions are dissolved, and Śiva is seen in the cosmos, hence also in the untouchable.

Thus, several pairs of identities are involved: (1) sannyāsī and cāṇḍāla; (2) Śaṅkara (supposedly an incarnation of Śiva)

[210] See *Manusmṛti* X.126: *na śūdre pātakaṁ kiñcit.*

and Śiva himself; and (3) one Jīva and another (devoid of *upādhis*). The encounter amounts to meeting oneself—ritualistically, theologically, and spiritually. This is how the category of abheda, or absence of distinctions, sheds light on the issue of social justice. So long as there are distinctions, discrimination will persist, or at least the potential for it. It is when all distinctions themselves have been erased that all distinctions can be ultimately removed, and the final possibility of full social justice emerges.

It now remains only to translate the message from transcendental into empirical terms. The challenge that Hindu thought poses to Hindu practice may be stated as follows: Ultimately the need for a theory of social justice will fade away if we do justice to our true spiritual identities, for then how one acts both realizes and reveals justice. At a less lofty level, the challenge Hindu *thought* poses to Hindu *practice* is to institutionalize the insight that the achievement of *equality* at the empirical level is the proper analogue to the achievement of Advaitic *identity* at the transcendental level. One's access to the peak of *identity* at the transcendental level is facilitated by an emphasis on equality at the empirical level, as one winds one's way up the magic mountain of spiritual progress.

XX

Āśrama

I

The āśrama dharma, or the doctrine of the stages of life, was also subjected to criticism by non-Hindus in the modern period, but this critique, unlike that of varṇa, did not quite stick. By and large, Hindus found little wrong with it, even as they acknowledged that much has gone wrong with the varṇa scheme. Nevertheless, its criticism provides an interesting point of entry into the topic.

The criticism basically stems from the charge that although four stages of life—that of the (1) student, (2) householder, (3) hermit, and (4) renunciant—are acknowledged, the stage or state of renunciation, or sannyāsa, was considered qualitatively superior, and that this imparts a world-denying character to the Hindu ethos. Modern Hinduism represents a living repudiation of this stand. Many of its leading figures were not renunciants, and even those who were, chose to live in the world rather than retire into a cave. Thus, such people as Rammohun Roy, Devendranath Tagore, and Keshub Chunder Sen did not renounce the world; Rāmakṛṣṇa and Vivekananda did, but continued to live in it—while Rāmakṛṣṇa was also married; Dayānanda Sarasvatī was a renunciant, but lived and moved in the world. Rabindranath Tagore openly questioned the ideal of renunciation in his poems,[211] while both Aurobindo and Radhakrishnan were married.

Mahatma Gandhi and Rāmakṛṣṇa, as they adopted an ascetic life style within a married state, should perhaps be considered 'hermits' rather than 'renunciants', and Gandhi in fact said so in so many words.[212] One could thus plausibly state that the world has been revalorized in modern Hinduism in terms of the āśrama scheme.

A much more significant development, however, is represented by the emergence of a subtler understanding of the concept that now pervades modern Hinduism, thanks to the popularity of the Bhagavadgītā.

A closer examination of the āśrama doctrine's division of human life into four stages reveals the fact that they represent graded manifestations of a more fundamental division of life into two orientations, or stages—one of engagement in the world (lasting until one turns fifty, so to say), and thereafter one of disengagement from the world. From this perspective, the life of a student constitutes a preparation for the life of the householder; while the life of a hermit constitutes a preparation for the life of a renunciant. It is this twofold movement that underlies the fourfold scheme of the āśrama.

The Sanskrit words which represent these two movements are pravṛtti, for engagement in the world, and nivṛtti, for disengagement from it. The initial understanding of the word had both physical and mental component. Thus, in the state of worldly engagement, one was physically present in the world of everyday life and also applied one's mind to it. Similarly, in the state of disengagement, one left the vortex of worldly activity in favour of the tranquility of a sylvan retreat and applied one's mind to spiritual concerns.

The realization gradually emerged in the tradition that pravṛtti and nivṛtti are, above all, states of the mind, rather

[211] See Hal W. French and Arvind Sharma, *Religious Ferment in Modern India*, New York: St. Martin's Press, 1981, p. 134.

[212] M.K. Gandhi, *An Autobiography: The Story of My Experiments with Truth*, Boston: Beacon Press, 1993, p. 206.

than physical locations. Thus, one could be in the world, but not of it, while living in it. Similarly, even though one might be physically living in a monastery, one's thinking could still be dominated by worldly concerns. It was thus possible to have nivṛtti in pravṛtti, and pravṛtti in nivṛtti, given the physical and mental connotations of these words, and the primacy of the mental one. The scheme of the four āśramas could thus be reduced to mental states, a position that modern Hinduism would identify as a central teaching of the Gītā.

We revert now to a consideration of the traditional scheme in a modern context.

II

The āśrama scheme of life has been hailed by some modern Hindu scholars as one of the great contributions of Hinduism to social thought. There may be some truth in this, as this doctrine enables us to look at life steadily, and view it holistically. Such appreciation, however, should not blind us to a subtle shift that is occurring in this doctrine, although it can be fully comprehended within the framework of the āśrama scheme itself. As is well-known, according to this doctrine 'there are four āśramas or stages in life: *brahmacarya* or a period of studentship, *gṛhastha* or the stage of a householder, *vānaprastha* or the stage of a forest-dweller, and *sannyāsa* or the life of renunciation.'[213] It was noted earlier that the first two āśramas, especially the crucial second, represent pravṛtti or engagement in the world, while the last two represent nivṛtti, or withdrawal from participation. What the Gītā says is that it is possible to practise pravṛtti in nivṛtti, and nivṛtti in pravṛtti—and the message seems to be catching on in modern Hinduism.

It would be apt, however, to now strike a slightly different note. Hinduism has often been associated with the twin institutions of varṇa and āśrama. The varṇa system, on account of

[213] Kane, P.V., *History of Dharmaśāstra*, Vol. V, Part II, Poona: Bhandarkav Oriental Research Institute, p. 1026.

its connection with the caste system—if the two are distinguished—or representing the caste system—if they are not—has come under strong criticism as being morally iniquitous, socially divisive, and politically enfeebling. Modern Hinduism, therefore, tends to be on the defensive while discussing the varṇa system, especially when it is identified with the caste system. Thus, as T.M.P. Mahadevan moves from a discussion of the varṇa to the āśrama system, he remarks: 'We are *on safer ground* when we consider the nature of āśrama-dharma (duties pertaining to stages of life).'[214]

This is not an isolated response. Unlike the varṇa system, the āśrama system continues to be ideologically, if not practically, popular in modern Hinduism. Edward Shils noted in 1961 how, among the Indian intellectuals, 'the third and fourth stages' continued 'to have tremendous power over those we interviewed.'[215] A survey of Indian students carried out in the later part of the same decade by Philip Ashby among the students of Andhra University of Waltair confirms the observation. Ashby writes: 'The surprising number of affirmative statements concerning the Āśramas was the most significant instance of evidence of a clinging to concepts of ideal action which were demonstrably not followed by the individuals and groups that signified their approval of such traditions. Many who expressed highly critical views of traditional Hindu practice and belief frequently also expressed the conviction that a revival of ancient ideals and forms in modern guise was of supreme importance to the well-being of contemporary Hinduism.'[216]

At the same time, however, it must be noted that the support for the system was far from unanimous. 'In a companion question about the practice of the four traditional stages of life (āśramas) in the modern world, 44 per cent felt they should be practiced. The twice-born men (that is, men who have the

[214] Mahadevan, T.M.P., *Outlines of Hinduism*, p. 75, emphasis added.

[215] Cited in Philip Ashby, *Modern Trends in Hinduism*, New York and London: Columbia University Press, 1974, p. 62, note 5.

[216] *Ibid.*, p. 62.

right to be invested with the sacred thread) in particular felt that the following of these stages—student, householder, hermit, and ascetic (sannyāsī)—was of importance in perpetuating the values of Hindu society as well as bringing spiritual fulfilment to the individuals involved. Two men and one woman had never heard of the āśramas. *The Untouchables were unanimous in their rejection of them.*'[217] A fissure in the āśrama system thus seems to run along varṇa lines. One must also take external forces at work into account alongside this internal division of opinion. Troy Wilson Organ instituted the following comparison in the 1970s between Western and Indian outlooks:

> Hinduism does not think of a man chiefly in terms of what he does to make a living, as is usually the case in the West. In the *āśrama* plan for life, earning a living occupies only the second period; during the first a Hindu is supported by those of his family who are in the second period, and during the third and fourth periods he is supported both by his previous earnings and by those of his family who are in the second period. The difference between the Western and the Hindu views of man can be illustrated by what is expected in answer to the question 'Who is he?' The answer expected in the West is an identification of his occupation, e.g., 'He is a carpenter...a farmer...a lawyer, etc.' In India, the proper Hindu reply would name his *jāti* and *gotra*, and perhaps his sect and language, e.g., 'He is a Bharadwaja Vadama Brahmin.' In other words, 'Who is he?' in Hinduism elicits a response about status.[218]

One might wonder whether, with the dissolution of varṇa and perhaps even āśrama in the traditional forms, this will continue to be the case.

[217] *Ibid.*, emphasis supplied.

[218] Wilson Organ, Troy, *The Hindu Quest for the Perfection of Man*, Athens: Ohio University, 1970, p. 232, note 112.

XXI

Puruṣārthas

Modern Hinduism has constellated the doctrine of the puruṣārthas in ways unknown to classical Hinduism. In some cases, the parallel holds—as when a materialist interpretation by Marxism is encountered. This is a flesh-and-bones encounter with the straw figure of the *Lokāyatas* that Hindu dialecticians used to set up as the *pūrvapakṣa* (the preliminary view to be subsequently refuted). In fact, Marxist scholars such as D. Chattopadhyaya[219] actually played the ideological game that way, and tried to demonstrate how Marxism was the 'crown' of Indian philosophical thought. Given the Hindu-Buddhist encounter in classical India, especially under Aśoka (third century BC), even the point that several different religious systems may try to define what is meant by dharma as a puruṣārtha is not unprecedented. Where modern Hinduism faced uncharted waters becomes clear when we ask the question: What are the goals to be achieved by society (*samājārtha*) as distinguished from the puruṣārthas? The idea of setting up a democratic, secular, socialist republic no doubt has practical implications for the individual, but its ideological implications are more far-reaching. What happens then to the goal

[219] Chattopadhyaya, D., *Lokāyata: A Study in Ancient Indian Materialism*, New Delhi: People's Publishing House, 1973.

of dharma if events take the course as anticipated by Hendrik Kraemer?

Logically speaking, secularism or secularity as the dominant trend of the modern outlook implies the atrophy of the religious constituent in human nature. By its inherent persistent drive to master the world and subject it to the quasi-omnipotence of human insight and manipulation, it impels at the same time towards a self-sufficient, purely profane anthropocentrism and towards a no less distinct self-alienation of man. It forces men automatically into an excessive preoccupation with the pursuit of worldly ends, with progress, with ever faster change. It generates a massive suggestion towards a purely immanent view of life. This *secular* immanentism must be stressed, because it presupposes and engenders (logically speaking) a religionless world. A world in which God is superfluous, squeezed out and absent. Superfluous even as a decent hypothesis. Also a world in which mind and spirit, that same human mind and spirit which are the creators of this overpowering tendency, seem to lose true capacity for religious directness.[220]

In fact, modern Hinduism (or secularism) is undergoing a major intellectual crisis at the moment on this issue.[221] We shall confine ourselves to the Hindu context, wherein the concept of the puruṣārthas itself has been attacked as a myth[222] in the sense that their fourfold classification contains elements of overlap and arbitrariness. There are at least three ways, however, in which this concept has its uses in modern Hinduism.

First, the fact that artha and kāma are fully acknowledged as goals of human endeavour has done much to negate the concept of Hinduism as a life-denying religion. It is sometimes argued that dharma is the pre-eminent category among the four puruṣārthas, for artha and kāma must be pursued subject to dharma[223] while mokṣa can sometimes be subsumed under

[220] Kraemer, Hendrik, *World Cultures and World Religions: The Coming Dialogue*, p. 347.

[221] See T.N. Madan, 'Whither Indian Secularism?', *Modern Asian Studies*, 27(3):667–97 (1993).

[222] Krishna, Daya, 'The Myth of the Puruṣārthas',in *Journal of Indian Council of Philosophical Research*, IV:1:1–13 (Autumn 1986).

[223] See Arvind Sharma, *The Puruṣārthas: A Study in Hindu Axiology*, East Lansing: Asian Studies Center, Michigan State University, 1982, *passim*.

dharma.[224] But even if one accepts such an interpretation, it is difficult to dismiss Hinduism as otherworldly, for its concept of dharma is quite this-worldly in its orientation.

A second way in which the doctrine of four puruṣārthas is helpful, flows ironically, from the attempts to deconstruct it by claiming that the range of human aspirations, in all their variety, cannot be encompassed by its fourfold grid. This point, however, finds a sympathetic echo in the tradition when it is sometimes claimed that the numerical values of 'four' or 'five' or 'seven' are an arithmetical shorthand for 'many'. If Hinduism itself confesses, in a way, the intractable plurality of human aspirations, then it is a tribute to its realism and, again, its life-affirming quality.

The third way in which the doctrine is helpful follows an opposite line of argument, and proposes that the real significance of the fourfold division of puruṣārthas lies in the fact that each of the four *can* be an independent and exclusive goal of human endeavour, but that human well-being—both individual and social—lies in their collective and harmonious pursuit. Such a perspective enables modern Hinduism to offer a critique of Marxism as being exclusively artha-centred, Freudism as exclusively kāma-centred, and Fundamentalism as narrowly dharma-centred, and therefore offering partial and flawed takes on human life—a position vindicated by recent historical developments.

[224] T. Embree, Anislie, *The Hindu Tradition*, New York: Random House, 1972, p. 78, note 1.

XXII

Vedas

Classical Hinduism accepted, by and large, the dogma of Vedic authority and infallibility as far as knowledge about dharma and mokṣa was concerned; and it did so on the basis of the claim that the Vedas were eternal and self-revealed—*nitya* and *apauruṣeya*.[225]

Modern Hinduism is inclined to take a somewhat different view in this matter. It is true that some of its modern representatives, such as Swāmī Dayānanda Sarasvatī, took a stand similar to the classical one. The modern position has, however, by and large moved away from the classical.

The classical doctrine of the verbal authority of the Vedas was itself verbal, and involved a theory of language. Modern Hinduism does not value the Vedas for any similar formal reason. It looks upon the Vedas as the record of the religious experience of seers, and hence of value—the scriptures of the other religions of the world could also be viewed in a similar light. There is thus a tendency in modern Hinduism to take into account all the scriptures of the world, and even consider them as Vedas, for not only do we know that portions of the

[225] Murty, K. Satchidananda, *Revelation and Reason in Advaita Vedānta*, New York: Columbia University Press, 1959, Chapter II.

Vedas have been lost,[226] but the Vedas are said to be infinite.[227] As Mahatma Gandhi asked: 'What was the meaning of saying that the Vedas were the inspired word of God? If they were inspired, why not also the Bible and the Koran?'[228]

Gandhi here expresses the Nyāya view that the Vedas are authoritative because they are the word of God. This view of the Vedas in itself reflects a modern orientation—for the dominant classical view as represented by the Mīmāṁsā school regarded the Vedas as self-revealed and eternal. Even in the context of this traditional view, modern Hinduism takes a somewhat modified position and tries to bring the human agency—and the role of experience—into the picture. Thus, M. Hiriyanna writes:

> But, theological considerations apart, it should be admitted that the truths for which the Veda stands, whether or not it is now possible to ascribe them to specific thinkers, should eventually be traced to some human source; and the fact seems to be implied in the description of those truths as having been *seen* by inspired sages (*ṛṣis*) of old. If it be so, the Veda also must be reckoned as communicating to us the results intuited by ancient sages. But there is a very important difference, as may be gathered from a condition which is sometimes laid down as essential to all 'revealed' teaching, viz. that it should have proved acceptable to the best minds (*mahājana*) of the community. This may appear to be only a begging of the question at issue, for non-Vedic tradition also claims to have been accepted by the best minds of the community. What, however, is meant by this new condition seems to be that, if a doubt arises as to the validity of the views handed down from the past, adherents of the present school appeal, as those of the other do not, to a community of minds which they have satisfied. Thus the standard here becomes eventually a society of men, and not an individual; and, by virtue of the objective status which it thus acquires, its deliverances are taken to possess an authority which cannot belong to those of anybody's private intuition. Herein

[226] Radhakrishnan, S. (ed.), *The Principal Upaniṣads*, London: George Allen & Unwin, 1953, p. 67.

[227] Mahadevan, T.M.P., *Outlines of Hinduism*, Bombay: Chetana Ltd., 1971, p. 39.

[228] *Gandhi's Autobiography* (tr.), Mahadev Desai, Washington, D.C. Public Affairs Press, 1948, p. 171.

may be said to lie the superiority of *śruti* to mere *smṛti*, in the sense given to it above. The Mīmāṁsā and the Vedānta are the systems that accept 'revelation,' in this sense, as the means to a knowledge of supersensuous truth.[229]

In fact, even when the dogma of Vedic authority is asserted in its strongest form, modern scholars try to dilute it as much as possible.

But it may be thought that the doctrine, however important the place it assigns to reason may be, is essentially dogmatic, because its truth is primarily to be known through revelation. That such a conclusion, however, does not follow will be seen when we remember the exact function of revelation. The aim here, as in the case of other Indian doctrines, is not merely to grasp the ultimate truth intellectually but to realize it in one's own experience. The scripture as such, being a form of verbal testimony, can however convey only mediate knowledge. To attain the ideal therefore meens to advance farther than merely comprehending the scriptural truth. Scriptural knowledge, accordingly, is not sufficient, though necessary; and like reason, it also therefore becomes only a subsidiary aid to the attainment of the goal. The Upanishads themselves declare that when a person has seen this truth for himself, he outgrows the need for the scriptures. 'There a father becomes no father; a mother, no mother; the world, no world; the gods, no gods; the Vedas, no Vedas.' Thus we finally get beyond both reason and revelation, and rest on direct experience (*anubhava*). Hence if Advaita is dogmatic, the dogma is there only to be transcended. Further, we should not forget that revelation itself goes back to the intuitive experience of the great seers of the past. It is that experience which is to be personally corroborated by the disciple.[230]

In the end then 'the ultimate court of appeal is plenary experience (*anubhava*). Scripture is valid because it reveals the nature of that experience.'[231]

The Sāṅkhya position on the Vedas might actually appeal to the modern Hindu mind in terms of the transmission and

[229] Hiriyanna, M., *The Essentials of Indian Philosophy*, London: George Allen & Unwin, 1948, p. 45.

[230] *Ibid.*, p. 173.

[231] Mahadevan, T.M.P., *op. cit.*, p. 144.

nature of the text. According to Sāṅkhya, the Vedas are apauruṣeya, but not nitya. They are apauruṣeya, or impersonal, in the sense that although the law of gravity was discovered by a person, the law itself is impersonal. But the Vedas are not eternal, because the chain of their transmission could be broken.[232] However, if we regard the spiritual insights themselves as both impersonal *and* eternal per se, even this possibility need not be considered.

One may thus accept the Vedas and their guidance, but not necessarily their dogmatic authority—this applies to the other scriptures of the world as well, which should also be read. Mahatma Gandhi sets the tone for modern Hinduism with the following words:

> The reader will note that I have purposely refrained from using the word divine origin in reference to the Vedas or any other scriptures. For I do not believe in the exclusive divinity of the Vedas. I believe the Bible, the Quran, and the Zend Avesta to be as much divinely inspired as the Vedas. My belief in the Hindu scriptures does not require me to accept every word and every verse as divinely inspired. Nor do I claim to have any first-hand knowledge of these wonderful books. But I do claim to know and feel the truths of the essential teaching of the scriptures. I decline to be bound by any interpretation, however learned it may be, if it is repugnant to reason or moral sense.[233]

It follows that the attitude of the modern Hindus to the Vedas, as their own specific scriptures, would be similar:

> The Hindu attitude to the Vedas is one of trust tempered by criticism, trust because the beliefs and forms which helped our fathers are likely to be of use to us also; criticism because, however valuable the testimony of past ages may be, it cannot deprive the present age of its right to inquire and sift the evidence. Precious as are the echoes of God's voice in the souls of men of long ago, our regard for them must be tempered by the recognition of the truth that God has never finished the revelation of His wisdom and love. Besides, our interpretation of

[232] Catterjee, Satischandra and Dhirendramohan Datta, *An Introduction to Indian Philosophy*, University of Calcutta, 1968, p. 279.

[233] M.K. Gandhi, *Hindu Dharma*, Ahmedabad: Navajivan Publishing House, 1950, p. 7.

religious experience must be in conformity with the findings of science. As knowledge grows, our theology develops. Only those parts of the tradition which are logically coherent are to be accepted as superior to the evidence of the senses, and not the whole tradition.[234]

The introduction of science in this passage is significant and identifies that strand in modern Hinduism which views the Vedas 'scientifically'.[235]

This attitude, which accords primacy to experience—be that of conscience, rationality, or spirituality—over scripture is carried over in modern Hinduism to the interpretation of other 'sacred' texts as well. Śaṅkara (ninth century) is a famous exegete whose writings are considered paradigmatic for Advaita Vedānta. Many tended to form the impression that the modern Advaitin saint, Ramaṇa Maharṣi (1879–1950), was his follower. Ramaṇa Maharṣi sets the record straight as follows:

D: Is Bhagavan's teaching the same as Shankara's?

B: Bhagavan's teaching is an expression of his own experience and realization. Others find that it tallies with Sri Shankara's.[236]

Mahatma Gandhi went so far as to say: 'I do most emphatically repudiate the claim (if they advance any such) of the present *shankaracharyas* and *shastris* to give a correct interpretation of the scriptures.'[237] And, as for Vedic authority he was once asked by Mr Mathews, a Christian interlocutor:

Where do you find the seat of authority?

Gandhiji: It lies here (pointing to his breast). I exercise my judgment about every scripture, including the Gita. I cannot let a scriptural text supersede my reason. Whilst I believe that the principal books are inspired, they suffer from a process of double distillation. Firstly, they

[234] Radhakrishnan, S., *The Hindu View of Life*, pp. 18–19.

[235] *Ibid.*, pp. 14–15.

[236] Osborne, Arthur (ed.), *The Teachings of Bhagavan Sri Ramana Maharshi in His Own Words*, Tiruvannamalai: Sri Ramanasramam, 1971, p. 11. D = Devotee; B = Bhagavan Ramaṇa Maharṣi.

[237] M.K. Gandhi, *Hindu Dharma*, p. 7.

come through a human prophet, and then through the commentaries of interpreters. Nothing in them comes from God directly. Mathew may give one version of one text, and John may give another. I cannot surrender my reason whilst I subscribe to divine revelation. And above all, 'the letter killeth, the spirit giveth life'. But you must not misunderstand my position. I believe in Faith also, in things where Reason has no place, e.g. the existence of God. No argument can move me from that faith, and like that little girl who repeated against all reason 'Yet we are seven', I would like to repeat, on being baffled in argument by a very superior intellect, 'Yet there is God'.[238]

[238] *Ibid.*, p. 34. For an excellent discussion of the role of the Veda in modern Hinduism also see Julius Lipner, *op. cit.*, Part I, Chapter 3.

❋

Glossary

Acarya Rajneesh (d. 1990): A modern guru who developed a system of giving instant *sannyāsa* to his followers and did much to narrow the gap between sex and spirituality.

Advaita Vedānta: The well-known school of Hindu thought which offers an absolutistic, as distinguished from a theistic, interpretation of the Hindu scriptures.

Annie Besant (1847–1933): Annie Besant, although of British extraction, adopted India as her home. She was active in the Theosophical Society and also served as its president. She Hinduized herself completely and also became the president of the Indian National Congress.

Anuloma: Hindu *Smṛtis* generally encourage men and women to marry a person from their own *varṇa*. If, however, a marriage takes place in which the husband belongs to a *varṇa* higher than the wife's (e.g. a *brāhmaṇa* man marrying a *kṣatriyas* woman) then the marriage is called *anuloma*. If the husband belongs to a lower *varṇa* than the wife it is called *pratiloma*. *Anuloma* marriages are preferable to *pratiloma* marriages. 'The former was "in accordance with the direction of the hair" (*anuloma*), smooth and natural, while the latter was "against the hair", or "brushing the wrong way" (*pratiloma*). This distinction is to be found in other societies; for instance in Victorian England the peer who married an actress rarely incurred the same scorn and ostracism as the lady who married the groom' (A. L. Basham, *The Wonder That Was India*, p. 147).

Arthaśāstra: The major surviving Hindu text on polity, attributed to Cāṇakya (also known as Kauṭilya), who is supposed to have masterminded the overthrow of the Nanda dynasty in the fourth century BCE, a fact also alluded to in the colophon of the text. The word also refers to the genre represented by the text.

Arya Samaj: A reform movement within modern Hinduism founded by Swami Dayānanda Sarasvatī (1824–83). It drew its inspiration from the Vedic legacy of Hinduism rather than from the West.

Bhāgavata-Purāṇa: The best-known of the eighteen Purāṇas which deals with the early life of Kṛṣna who appears in the *Mahābhārata* as an adult. The text is specially known for its depiction of the love of the milkmaids or *gopīs* for Kṛṣṇa.

Bharatanāṭyam: Literally the dance of Bharata viz. a dance performed in accordance to the rules laid down in Bharata's *Nāṭyaśāstra*, a text assigned to a period stretching from the second century BCE to the second century CE, which offers the classical formulation of Hindu dance, drama, and music. *Bharatanāṭyam* specially refers to a form of classical dance in contemporary times, which is lineally descended from the artistic practices of the Devadāsīs.

Brāhmo Samaj: A reform movement within modern Hinduism, founded by Raja Rammohun Roy (1772/4–1833), which reflected modern influences.

Devadāsī: The word literally means a slave or servant of God and denotes the practice according to which women were dedicated to the temples, to be raised in a way which made them proficient in worshipping the deity through the cultivation of the arts, specially dance. It was denounced by the British as a form of temple prostitution.

Edward Digby Baltzell (1915–1996): He was a professor of sociology at the University of Pennsylvania, and is the author of *The Protestant Establishment: Aristocracy and Caste* (1964).

Faxian: The Chinese traveller, otherwise known as Fa-hien or Fa-shien, who visited India from CE 399–414 and left an account of his visit which is a valuable source of information regarding life in India during the Gupta period.

Freudism: The school of psychoanalysis associated with Sigmund Freud (1856–1939) which emphasizes the role of unconscious, and specially sexual, drives in explaining human behavior.

Fundamentalism: An interpretation of a religious tradition which emphasizes a literal meaning of the scriptures and a conservative morality in reaction to its encounter with modernity. Fundamentalism should be distinguished from orthodoxy which is a tradition's response to loss of piety, while fundamentalism is a response to loss of power.

Gopīs: The milkmaids of Vṛndāvana: Kṛṣṇa's dalliance with these milkmaids in his childhood and early youth is a leitmotif of romantic devotional poetry.

Guptas: A political dynasty of ancient India which ruled over North India in the fourth and fifth centuries AD. The period of their rule is said to have marked the acme of classical Hindu culture.

Jayanta: Jayanta, or Jayanta Bhaṭṭa, flourished in the ninth century AD. He belonged to the Nyāya school of Hindu thought and is one of the leading thinkers of ancient India. His views on the nature of revealed texts are strikingly modern in their catholicity.

Kātyāyana: The name signifies a *smṛti* or law book attributed to Kātyāyana; not to be confused with the grammarian of the third century BCE with the same name. P. V. Kane assigns it to a period between the fourth and sixth centuries AD.

Mahānirvāṇatantra: A Tāntrika text, whose date and origins are a matter of much debate among scholars. It presents the form of *Śākta-tantra* known as *kaula*, derived from the word *kula*, which is how *Brahman* is referred to in these texts, in which spiritual advancement culminates in the *kaula-mārga* after the other six preceding *ācāras*—listed as Veda, Vaiṣṇava, Śaiva, Dakṣiṇa, Vāma, and Siddhānta—have been traversed. The text is remarkable for its message of gender and caste equality.

Manusmṛti: No less than forty-six *smṛtis* or law-books are known in Hindu literature although the texts of all of them are not available. The *Manusmṛti*, assigned to a period from second century BCE to second century CE, is traditionally considered the most authoritative among them.

Marxism: The interpretation of human history as essentially a history of class conflict, as propounded by Karl Marx (1818–83).

Mātsyanyāya: The expression literally means (big) fish eat (small) fish and is a metaphor for anarchy, in the spirit of dog-eat-dog and the war of all against all. It represents the state of affairs which rendered the institution of kingship, as symbolizing political order, necessary.

Nāma-japa: The word literally means murmuring the name, that is to say, the name of God. It was an important expression of piety in medieval Hinduism.

Parva: A book or canto in the Mahābhārata, which contains eighteen *parvas* in all.

Puruṣasūkta: This is how a hymn of the ṚgVeda (X.90) is often referred to on account of the fact that it describes the emergence of the cosmic, physical, and social order from the primeval *puruṣa* or macranthropus through a primeval (self-) sacrifice.

Rāmacaritamānāsa: This text, sometimes also transliterated as *Rāmcaritmānas*, is a rendering in Hindi of the famous epic, Rāmāyaṇa, by Tulsīdās in the seventeenth century, and is immensely popular in the Hindi-speaking areas of India.

Rāmakṛṣṇa Paramahaṁsa (1836–86): A major figure in the Hindu renaissance of the nineteenth and twentieth centuries who is credited with having restored Hindu self-confidence, specially through the activities of his disciple Vivekānanda (1863–1902). Rāmakṛṣṇa is also noteworthy for vindicating the neo-Hindu view through personal mystical experience that all religions are valid pathways to the Divine.

Ramana Maharshi (1879–1950): A major exponent of experiential Advaita Vedānta in the twentieth century.

Rāmānuja (1017–1137): A famous Hindu philosopher who differs from Śaṅkara in identifying theism rather than absolutism as the purport of Hindu sacred literature. He placed the devotional songs of Tamil Vaiṣṇava saints as compiled in the *Nālayira-Prabandham* on par with the Upaniṣads, thereby leading to his system being designated as *Ubhayavedānta* or twofold Vedānta.

S. Radhakrishnan (1888–1975): A major interpreter of Hinduism in and for modern times, who was also a prominent figure in public life and President of India from 1962–7.

Śaṅkara: A famous Hindu philosopher who used to be assigned to c. AD 788–820 but for whom the revised dates of c. AD 650–82 have been recently recommended. He is the paradigmatic expounder of the school of Hindu philosophy known as Advaita Vedānta, formulated by him in the course of his commentaries on its three foundational texts: (1) the Upaniṣads; (2) the Brahmasūtra, and (3) the Bhagavadgītā.

Śaṅkara-Digvijaya: A text which celebrates the triumphal march of Śaṅkara as he overcomes adversaries in debate to establish his system of philosophy as the normative expression of Hinduism. Many such texts exist, and the fourteenth century BC/AD text by Mādhava is perhaps the best known.

Śuṅgas: A dynasty which ruled over much of North India from c. 186

to c. 73 BC when India was subject to several invasions from the north-west by outsiders, including the Greeks and the Bactrians.

Sharī'ah: The word literally means the way to the watering-hole and connotes the divine blueprint regarding the way human life should be lived and human affairs be conducted, in accordance with the will of God as understood in Islam.

Sir Francis Younghusband (1863–1942): Sir Younghusband led the British expedition to Lhasa in 1904 but thereafter turned a new leaf and became interested in spirituality. He founded the World Congress of Faiths.

Sister Nivedita (d. 1911): An Irish follower of Swami Vivekānanda, otherwise known as Margaret Noble, whose devotion to the cause of Hinduism made a deep impression on the Indian people.

Swami Vivekānada (1863–1902): The outstanding disciple of Rāmakṛṣṇa Paramahaṁsa, who broadcast his message of the validity of all religions in the West, while defending Hinduism against the attacks on it, specially by Christians and Christian missionaries.

Twice-born: The English term into which the Sanskrit word *dvija* is translated, and which has gained considerable currency on its own. It refers to the understanding that undergoing the ritual for initiation into Vedic studies constitutes a rebirth. The concept of the twice-born should not be confused with the concept of a 'born again' Christian in Christianity.

Udayana: A famous Nyāya thinker of ancient India who flourished in the tenth century BC. His proofs of the existence of God have aroused much interest.

Upanayana: The word literally means 'taking one close', that is, taking the young boy ready for pursuing Vedic studies close to the teacher for being initiated into them. The boy is invested with a sacred thread as part of the initiation.

Veda: Nitya *and* Apauruṣeya: The Vedas are described as *nitya* or eternal and *apuruṣeya* or without any known author, human or divine, in orthodox Vedantic Hindu understanding. In this conception, the text of the Veda never came into being but has existed from the beginning of time and it is spelled out by Brahmā at the beginning of each aeon. This apotheosis of the Veda, as it were, seems to have been the Hindu response to attacks on it by the Buddhists, the Jainas, and the Indian Materialists.

Vinoba Bhave (1895–1982): Considered by some as the spiritual successor of Mahatma Gandhi, Vinoba Bhave launched a movement for the voluntary donation of land for the landless by those who owned it in excess of their needs. This was called *bhūdāna*. He also tried to contribute to the Gandhian legacy of austerity and charity in many other ways.

Viśiṣṭādvaita Vedānta: A well-known school of Hindu thought which offers a theistic, as distinguished from an absolutistic, interpretation of Hindu scriptures.

Vyāsa: The name signifies a *smṛti* or law book attributed to Vyāsa; not to be confused with the putative author of the Mahābhārata with the same name. P. V. Kane assigns it to a period between the second and fifth century AD.

Bibliography

Altekar, A.S., 1962, *The Position of Women in Hindu Civilization*, Delhi: Motilal Banarsidass.

Ambedkar, B.R., 1946, *Who Were the Shudras?*, Bombay: Thackers.

——, 1992, *Writings and Speeches*, Bombay: Education Department, Government of Maharashtra, Vol. 11.

Ashby, Philip, 1974, *Modern Trends in Hinduism*, New York and London: Columbia University Press.

Babb, Lawrence A., 1986, *Redemptive Encounters: Three Modern Styles in the Hindu Tradition*, Berkeley: University of California Press.

de Bary, William Theodore (ed.), 1958, *Sources of Indian Tradition*, New York and London: Columbia University Press.

Basham, A.L., 1967, 'Hinduism', in *The Concise Encyclopedia of Living Faiths*, R.C. Zaehner (ed.), Boston: Beacon Press.

——, 1999 [1954], *The Wonder that Was India*, New Delhi: Rupa & Co.

Beckerledge, Gwilym, 2000, 'Swami Akhandananda's *Sevavrata* (Vow of Service) and the Earliest Expressions of Service to Humanity in the Ramakrishna Math and Mission', in *Gurus and Their Followers: New Religious Reform Movements in Colonial India*, Antony Copley (ed.), New Delhi: Oxford University Press.

Bhargava, Rajeev, 1998, *Secularism and Its Critics*, Delhi: Oxford University Press.

Bhattacharyya, Batuknath, 1943, *The Kalivarjyas or Prohibitions in the Kali Age*, Calcutta: University of Calcutta.

Bhattacharyya, Bhabatosh (tr.), 1973, *Daṇḍaviveka of Vardhamāna Upādhyay* , Calcutta: The Asiatic Society.

Bose, Sugata and Ayesha Jalal, 1998, *Modern South Asia: History, Culture, Political Economy*, New Delhi: Oxford University Press.

Bowes, Pratima, 1977, *The Hindu Religious Tradition: A Philosophical Approach*, London: Routledge & Kegan Paul.

Boyd, R., 1979, *An Introduction to Indian Christian Theology*, Madras: Christian Literature Society.

Braveman, Amy M., 2004, 'The Interpretations of Gods: Do Leading Religious Scholars Err in Their Analysis of Hindu Texts', in *University of Chicago Magazine* 97:2:33–6.

Brooke, Tal, 1979, *Sai Baba: Lord of the Air*, New Delhi: Vikas Publishing Company.

Campbell, Joseph, 1974, *The Mythic Image*, Princeton N.J.: Princeton University Press.

Chatterjee, Bankim Chandra, 1977, *The Essentials of Dharma*, Calcutta: Sribhumi Publishing Co.

Chatterjee, Satischandra and Dhirendramohan Datta, 1968, *An Introduction to Indian Philosophy*, Calcutta: Calcutta University Press.

Chattopadhyaya, D., 1973, *Lokāyata: A Study in Ancient Indian Materialism*, New Delhi: People's Publishing House.

Chaudhuri, Narayan, 1973, *Maharshi Devendranath Tagore*, New Delhi: Sahitya Akademi.

Chaudhuri, Nirad C., 1979., *Hinduism: A Religion to Live By*, New York: Oxford University Press.

Chirol, Valentine, 1910, *Indian Unrest*, London: Macmillan & Co.

The Complete Works of Sister Nivedita, (Four vols.), 1967, Calcutta: Ramakrishna Sarada Mission.

The Complete Works of Swami Vivekananda (Vol. I), (Mayavati Memorial Edition), 1986, Calcutta: Advaita Ashram.

The Cultural Heritage of India, (Four vols.), 1958, Calcutta: The Ramakrishna Mission Institute of Culture.

Dandekar, R.N., 1965, 'Role of Man in Hinduism', in *The Religion of the Hindus*, Kenneth W. Morgan (ed.), New York: The Ronald Press Company.

Devaraja, N.K., 1975, *Hinduism and the Modern Age*, New Delhi: Islam and the Modern Age Society.

Diehl, Anita, 1978, *Periyar E.V. Ramaswami: The Study of the Influence of a Personality in Contemporary South India*, Bombay: B.I. Publications.

Dirks, Nicholas B., 2001, *Castes of Mind: Colonialism and the Making of Modern India*, Princeton and Oxford: Princeton University Press.

Durant, Will, 1926, *The Story of Philosophy*, New York: Garden City Publishing Co.

Embree, Ainslie T., 1972, *The Hindu Tradition.* New York: Random House.

———, (ed.), 1988, *Sources of Indian Tradition,* New York: Columbia University Press.

Flood, Gavin, 1996, *An Introduction to Hinduism,* Cambridge: Cambridge University Press.

Foulston, Lynn, 2002, *At the Feet of the Goddess: The Divine Feminine in Local Hindu Religion,* Brighton and Portland, Oregon: Sussex Academic Press.

French, Hal W. and Arvind Sharma, 1981, *Religious Ferment in Modern India,* New York: St. Martin's Press.

Fromm, Erich, 1950, *Psychoanalysis and Religion,* New Haven: Yale University Press.

Gandhi, M.K., 1950. *Hindu Dharma,* Ahmedabad: Navajivan Publishing House.

———, 1948, *The Story of My Experiments with Truth,* Mahadev Desai (tr.), Washington, D.C.: Public Affairs Press.

Ganguli, K.M. (tr.), 1981, *The Mahābhārata of Krishna-Dwaipayana-Vyasa* (fourth edition), New Delhi: Munshiram Manoharlal Publishers.

Godman, David (ed.), 1985, *The Teachings of Ramana Maharshi,* London and New York: Arkana.

Goldman, Robert P. (tr.), 1984, *The Rāmāyaṇa of Vālmīki,* (Vol. I), Princeton, N.J.: Princeton University Press.

Gopalkrishnan, M.D., 1991, *Periyar: Father of the Tamil Race,* Madras: Emerald.

Griswold, H.D., 1971, *The Religion of the Rigveda,* Delhi: Motilal Banarsidass.

Halbfass, Wilhelm, 1988, *India and Europe: An Essay in Understanding,* Albany, NY: State University of New York Press.

Harris, Ishwar C., 1982, *Radhakrishnan: Profile of a Universalist,* Calcutta: Minerva Associates [Publications] Pvt. Ltd.

Hiriyanna, M., 1949, *The Essentials of Indian Philosophy,* London: George Allen & Unwin.

Jaffrelot, Christophe, 1996, *The Hindu Nationalist Movement in India,* New York: Columbia University Press.

Jain, H.M., 1995, 'Casteism and the Struggle for Social Justice', Unpublished paper.

Joshi, Shashi and Bhagwan Josh, 1994, *Struggle for Hegemony in India 1920–1947,* New Delhi: Sage Publications.

Joshi, Tarkateertha Laxmanshastri, 2001, *Development of Indian Culture: Vedas to Gandhi,* S.R. Nene (tr.), Mumbai: Loka Vangmaya Griha.

Kane, P.V., 1962, *History of Dharmaśāstra* (Five Vols), Poona: Bhandarkar Oriental Research Institute.

Kerry, John, 2000, *India: A History*, New York: Atlantic Monthly Press.

Kinsley, David R., 1982, *Hinduism: A Cultural Perspective* (second edition), Englewood Cliffs, New Jersey: Prentice Hall.

Klostermaier, Klaus K., 1994, *A Survey of Hinduism* (second edition), Albany, N.Y.: State University of New York Press.

Kraemer, Hendrik., 1960, *World Cultures and World Religions: The Coming Dialogue*, London: Lutterworth Press.

Krishna, Daya, 1986, 'The Myth of the Puruṣārthas', in *Journal of Indian Council of Philosophical Research* 4:1:1–13, Autumn.

Lefeber, Rosalind (tr.), 1994, *Rāmāyaṇa of Vālmīki*, Vol. IV, Princeton, N.J.: Princeton University Press.

Lipner, Julius, 1999, *Brahmabandhab Upadhyay: The Life and Thought of a Revolutionary*, Delhi: Oxford University Press.

———, 1994, *Hindus: Their Religious Beliefs and Practices*. London and New York: Routledge.

Lyall, Sarah, 1999, 'Hoddle, Coach of England, Is Dismissed', in The *New York Times*, 3 February.

Madan, T.N., 1993, 'Whither Indian Secularism', in *Modern Asian Studies* 27(3):667–97.

Mahadevan, T.M.P., 1971, *Outlines of Hinduism*, Bombay: Chetana Limited.

Majumdar, R.C. (ed.), 1952, *The Vedic Age*, London: George Allen & Unwin Ltd.

Mani, Vettam, 1975, *Purāṇic Encyclopedia*, Delhi: Motilal Banarsidass.

Mannumel, Thomas, S.J., 1991, *The Advaita of Vivekananda: A Philosophical Appraisal*, Madras: T.R. Publications Pvt. Ltd.

Menski, Werner F., 2003, *Hindu Law: Beyond Tradition and Modernity*, New Delhi: Oxford University Press.

Michaels, Axel, 2004, *Hinduism Past and Present* (trans. by Barbara Harshav), Princeton and Oxford: Princeton University Press.

Miller, Joe & Guinevere (eds), 1988, *The Spiritual Teachings of Ramana Maharshi*, Boston and London: Shamabhala.

Mudaliar, A. Devaraj, compiler, 1978, *Gems from Bhagavan*, Tiruvannamalai, Sri Ramanasramam.

Muir, J., 1972, *Original Sanskrit Texts*, Part I, Delhi: Oriental Publishers.

Murphet, Howard, 1978, *Sai Baba Avatar*, Delhi: Macmillan.

Murty, K. Satchidananda, 1959, *Revelation and Reason in Advaita Vedānta*, New York: Columbia University Press.

———, 1993, *Vedic Hermeneutics*, Delhi: Motilal Banarsidass.

Murty, K. Satchidananda and Ashok Vohra, 1989, *Radhakrishnan: His Life and Ideas*, Delhi: Ajanta Publications.

Neill, Stephen, 1970, *The Story of the Christian Church in India and Pakistan*, Grand Rapids, Michigan: William B. Eerdmanns Publishing Company.

Nikhilananda, Swami (tr.), 1952, *The Gospel of Sri Ramakrishna*, New York: Ramakrishna-Vivekananda Center.

Nirvedananda, Swami, 1969, *Hinduism at a Glance*, Calcutta: Ramakrishna Mission.

O'Hanlon, Rosalind, 1985, *Caste, Conflict, and Ideology: Mahatma Jyotirao Phule and Low Caste Protest in Nineteenth Century Western India*, Cambridge: Cambridge University Press.

Oldenberg, Veena Talwar, 2002, *Dowry Murder: The Imperial Origins of a Cultural Crime*, New York: Oxford University Press.

Oldmeadow, Harry, 2002, *Journeys East: 20th Century Western Encounters*, Bloomington, Indiana: World Wisdom.

Olivelle, Patrick, 1993, *The Āśrama System: The History and Hermeneutics of a Religious Institution*, New York: Oxford University Press.

Olson, Carl, 1990, *The Mysterious Play of Kalī: An Interpretive study of Rāmakṛṣṇa*, Atlanta, Georgia: Scholars Press.

Omvedt, Gail, 2003, *Buddhism in India: Challenging Brahmanism and Caste*, New Delhi: Sage Publications.

Organ, Troy Wilson, 1970, *The Hindu Quest for the Perfection of Man*, Athens: Ohio University.

———, 1974, *Hinduism: Its Historical Development*, Woodbury, New York: Barron's Educational Series Inc.

Osborne, Arthur (ed.), 1971, *The Teachings of Bhagavan Sri Raman Maharshi in His Own Words*, Tiruvannamalai: Sri Ramanasramam.

———, 1995 [1970], *Ramana Maharshi and the Path of Self-Knowledge*, York Beach, Maine: Samuel Weiser Inc.

Palmer, Susan and Arvind Sharma, 1993, *The Rajneesh Papers: Studies in a New Religious Movement*, Delhi: Motilal Banarsidass.

Panda, K.B., 1977, *Sanatana Dharma and Law*, Cuttack: Naitika Punaruthan Samiti.

Pande, Govindra Chandra, 1994, *Life and Thought of Śaṅkarācārya*, Delhi: Motilal Banarsidass.

Payne, Robert, 1969, *The Life and Death of Mahatma Gandhi*, New York: E.P. Dutton.

Pollock, Sheldon, 1993, 'Rāmāyaṇa and the Political Imagination of India', *The Journal of Asian Studies* 52:2:261–97 (1993).

Preston, James J., 1987, 'Goddess Worship: Theoretical Perspectives', in *The Encyclopedia of Religion*, Vol. 6, Mircea Eliade, editor in chief, New York: Macmillan Publishing Company.

Pyarelal, 1958, *Mahatma Gandhi: The Last Phase*, Ahmedabad: Navajivan Publishing House.

Radhakrishnan, S., 1927, *The Hindu View of Life*, London: George Allen & Unwin.

———, (ed.), 1953, *The Principal Upaniṣads*, London: George Allen & Unwin.

———, (tr.), 1960, *The Brahma Sūtra: The Philosophy of the Spiritual Life*, London: George Allen & Unwin.

Rajgopalachari, C., 1964, *Sri Ramakrishna Upaniṣad*, Madras: Sri Ramakrishna Math.

Ramaswamy, Sumathi, 1999, 'Sanskrit for the Nation', *Modern Asian Studies* 33:2:339–81.

Ranikkar, K.M. 1961, *Hindu Society at the Cross Roads*, Bombay: Asia Publishing House.

Renou, Louis, 1951, *The Nature of Hinduism* (trans. Patrick Evans), New York: Walker & Co.

Richman, Paula (ed.), 2000, *Questioning Rāmāyaṇas: A South Asian Tradition*, Berkeley: University of California Press.

Roodurmun, P.S., 2002, *Bhāmatī and Vivaraṇa Schools of Advaita Vedānta: A Critical Approach*, Delhi: Motilal Banarsidass.

Saradananda, Swami, 1952, *The Great Master* (tr. by Swami Jagadananda), Madras: Sri Ramakrishna Math.

Sarma, D.S., 1956, *Hinduism Through the Ages*, Bombay: Bharatiya Vidya Bhavan.

Sen, K.M., 1963, *Hinduism*, Harmondsworth, U.K.: Penguin.

Sharma, Arvind, 1982, *The Puruṣārthas: A Study in Hindu Axiology*, East Lansing: Asian Studies Center, Michigan State University.

———, 1998, *The Concept of Universal Religion in Modern Hindu Thought*, London: Macmillan.

———, 2002, *Modern Hindu Thought: The Essential Texts*, New Delhi: Oxford University Press.

———, (ed.), 2003, *The Study of Hinduism*, Columbia, South Carolina: University of South Carolina Press.

Sharma, Ram Sharan, 1958, *Śūdras in Ancient India*, Delhi: Motilal Banarsidass.

Sharpe, Eric J., 1970, 'Anthropology', in A Dictionary of Comparative Religion, S.G.F. Brandon (ed.), New York: Macmillan Publishing company.

———, 1985, *The Universal Gītā*, London: Duckworth.
———, 2003, 'The Study of Hinduism—The Setting', in *The Study of Hinduism*, Arvind Sharma (ed.), Columbia, South Carolina: University of South Carolina Press.
Smith, David, 2003, *Hinduism and Modernity*, Malden, MA: Blackwell Publishing House.
Smith, Huston, 1991, *The World's Religions*, San Francisco: Harper.
Smith, Wilfred Cantwell, 1963, *The Meaning and End of Religion*, New York: The Macmillan Company.
Svāmī, Pūjyaśrī Chandraśekharendra Sarasvatī, 1996, *Hindu Dharma: The Universal Way of Life*, Mumbai: Bharatiya Vidya Bhavan.
Tirtha, Swami Bharati Krishna, 1985, *Sanathan Dharma*, Bombay: Bharatiya Vidya Bhavan.
van Buitenen, J.A.B. (tr.), 1973, *The Mahābhārata*, Chicago and London: The University of Chicago Press.
Walker, Benjamin, 1968, *The Hindu World*, New York: Frederick A. Praeger.
Williams, George M., 1974, *The Quest for Meaning of Svāmī Vivekānanda: A Study in Religious Change*, Chico, California: New Horizons Press.
Words of Anandamayi Ma, 1971, Varanasi: S.S. Anandamayee Sangha.
Yinger, Milton J., 1970, *The Scientific Study of Religion*, London: The Macmillan Company.
Zimmer, Heinrich, 1962, *Myths and Symbols in Indian Art and Civilization*, Joseph Campbell (ed.), New York and Evanston: Harper & Row.
Zysk, Kenneth G. (ed.), 1989, *The Origins and Development of Classical Hinduism (by) A.L. Basham*, Boston: Beacon Press.

Periodicals

Time, 15 February 1999.
Times of India, 31 August 1992.

Index